Welsh Canals
– then and now

First edition: April 1998
© Dennis Needham and Y Lolfa Cyf. 1998

ISBN: 0 86243 421 1

Maps and Photographs by Elizabeth Fowler

Printed and published in Wales by:
Y Lolfa Cyf., Talybont, Ceredigion, SY24 5AP
e-mail ylolfa@ylolfa.com
world-wide web http://www.ylolfa.com
tel (01970) 832 304
fax 832 782
isdn 832 813

Welsh Canals
– then and now

DENNIS NEEDHAM

yl Lolfa

Contents

For Stella

Introduction

This book is far from being the definitive text on Welsh canal history. Many learned scholars have researched the complete story in intimate detail and the results of their labours are chronicled for all who want to search out the minutiae of this wonderful transport system.

What will be found between these covers is a look at each canal in Wales that offers something for today's seeker of industrial archaeology, the walker or explorer, or anyone with an interest in this fascinating floating transport system that was fundamental to the development of industrial Wales.

The **Then ...** section gives a greatly abridged story of the development of each of the chosen navigations. The reasons for its proposal and construction, together with an insight into day to day operation are examined. The personalities and, sometimes, villains receive mention, as do the users. Where canals cross into England, the total history is included. Each canal has its own chapter and appears in chronological order of construction.

Following this history, a **And Now ...** section guides you on an exploration of what remains. Details of what is still there to be seen are given complete with map references. Some, like parts of the Neath or the Monmouthshire & Brecknock are still navigable. Others, the Aberdare is probably the best example, have virtually disappeared. This time, with cross-border canals, only the lengths within the Principality are included.

Then, included in Chapter Three is a fictional account of what working life might have been like in those long-gone days.

Most of the canals built in Wales are no longer operational. The advent of railways after half a century of waterway monopoly produced a transport system that was far more efficient. By the end of the nineteenth century, the whole system was effectively moribund, trade lost to the iron road.

Restoration work is in progress on some canals, and it is not beyond the bounds of possibility that what is dead at the time of writing may well become a vibrant waterway in the future. The only thing that does seem certain is that any canal today will be offered for recreation use only. The days of carrying are almost certainly gone for ever.

But whether the canal is full of boats, a foetid ditch or merely a dry depression in the ground, there will be some fascinating industrial architecture to be seen and admired. Use this guide to find it. Even along closed canals, the towing path is often still intact and offers fine walking. Frequently, this can be in the form of a one-way walk, using public transport for the return leg. Where this is possible, details are given.

Explore and enjoy, and then marvel at the wonderful examples of engineering and ingenuity that went into creating the canals of Wales.

Acknowledgements

My gratitude to Josephine Jeremiah for allowing her story "Boat Boy on the Glamorganshire Canal" to adorn Chapter Three. Ian Milne was a great help in compiling Chapter Four and Clive Reed provided invaluable help in Chapter Eight. Carol King for her painstaking proofreading and Elizabeth whose skill with lens and pen illustrate these words.

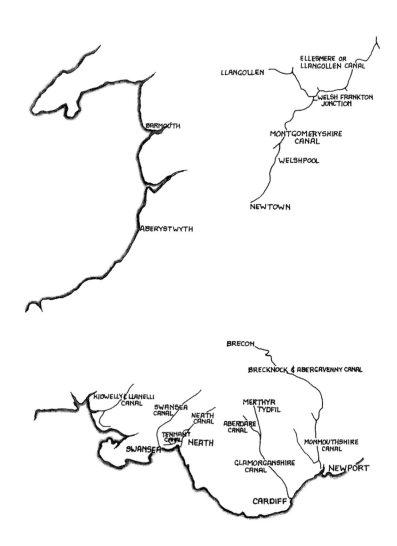

BARMOUTH

ABERYSTWYTH

LLANGOLLEN

ELLESMERE OR
LLANGOLLEN CANAL

WELSH FRANKTON
JUNCTION

MONTGOMERYSHIRE
CANAL

WELSHPOOL

NEWTOWN

BRECON

BRECKNOCK & ABERGAVENNY CANAL

KIDWELLY & LLANELLI
CANAL

SWANSEA
CANAL

NEATH
CANAL

MERTHYR
TYDFIL

ABERDARE
CANAL

TENNANT
CANAL

NEATH

SWANSEA

MONMOUTHSHIRE
CANAL

GLAMORGANSHIRE
CANAL

NEWPORT

CARDIFF

1. The Canal Age in Wales

The principal inland navigation developments in Wales came somewhat later than to the rest of the British mainland. This was much more to do with adverse terrain than lack of enterprise. Indeed, of that there was much.

It was the era of William Pitt the Younger in England and George Washington in the United States, still only a decade on from the Revolution. On the continent, the French Revolutionary wars were about to begin. At home, George III was on the throne, still relatively sane and working with the Tory party who had ousted the Whigs and would rule for half a century. This was the political backdrop to the dawning Canal Age, an age that would for ever change the face of this land.

In the mid-eighteenth century there were several small artificial navigations created in west Wales. All were designed to link collieries with the coast, all were short, and none played any significant part in the subsequent development of the main canals.

Up to two centuries ago, transport was a nightmare. Roads were rudimentary, water carriage restricted to rivers, railways still a distant dream. The sole criterion for manufacturing was to locate close to sources of raw materials.

Wood, limestone and iron ore – the basics of ironmaking – were to be found in the area now roughly traversed by the A465 Heads of the Valleys road, centred on Merthyr Tydfil. Consequently, several ironworks had been established there. As techniques improved, coal, also found locally, was used to replace charcoal. The number and size of iron works soon multiplied. Soon, Merthyr would become the world centre for iron production.

But, whilst increased productivity was fine in itself, it was nothing without the wherewithal to move finished goods to customers; industry was still thwarted by a lack of transport. Roads were ineffective at best; impassable for the rest.

In an effort to improve transit times and weights, the ironmasters and industrialists had invested in turnpike roads. These were controlled by gates at which point the users had to pay their toll. To protect against illicit use, vertical spikes were used. These could be "turned" out of the way by the toll keeper, thus allowing passage.

Whilst this system worked well within its limits, it was just not possible to handle the tonnages involved. At this point in history, John McAdam had yet to invent his tar-based process for surfacing roads and the system of (at best) compacted stone was woefully inadequate for the demands placed upon it.

Thus was the stage set for the final piece in the jigsaw that was to become known as the Industrial Revolution. Many of the same men who had been involved with the turnpikes had the foresight to look at canals, then making an early impression in England.

The general consensus amongst scholars is that one Francis Homfray provided the impetus that saw south Wales burst into the Canal Age. Together with his sons, Francis arrived in Merthyr Tydfil in 1782 and two years later opened an ironworks in the town at Penydarren. He had business connections in the Midlands, and had seen the incredible benefits accruing to companies who used the Staffordshire and Worcestershire canal.

The engineer Thomas Dadford was employed by that canal and known to Homfray. Thus, it was only natural that Homfray should approach him with details of a proposed canal from Merthyr Tydfil to Cardiff. Dadford accepted the post of Engineer, and contracted to build the canal, bringing his son Thomas and Thomas Sheasby to help.

News of this development spread rapidly. To the west, a canal seemed the ideal solution to similar transport problems being experienced in the Vale of Neath. The Neath Canal was proposed. This would run for thirteen miles (20.8km) north east to Glyn-Neath.

In the area of (now) Gwent, the ironfounders of Nantyglo and Blaenavon were also taking a keen interest in developments. The Monmouthshire Canal was the outcome. Their Act was passed in 1792. Francis Homfray's son Jeremiah, who had ironworks interest at Ebbw Vale, became a shareholder in this enterprise.

Immediately following that, The Brecknock and Abergavenny Canal was proposed. This would have run from Caerleon to Gilwern. Wiser counsels were to prevail however, and eventually the line would run from Brecon to Pontymoile, there to make an end-on connection with the Monmouthshire.

The Tawe valley saw the last of the great Welsh canals to be built. A Swansea Canal Act was granted in 1794 and the canal was built for just over 15 miles (24.1km) up the valley to Heneuadd.

By being a few years behind the main English canals, the engineers engaged to construct the Welsh waterways were able to draw on the experience of those who had gone before. There were no watershed canals in the country; all ran along valleys.

There were vast numbers of locks, but they all faced the same way. Several staircase flights were needed. These ensured a sharp fall (or rise) in a short distance by using a single gate between two or more chambers. This precluded the need for a pound between locks long enough to hold a head of water. Tunnels were a rarity in Wales. Only six were built and the longest was a mere 375 yards (343m). This was at Ashford near Talybont on the Brecknock and Abergavenny line.

As will be seen, most canal construction in Wales was carried out by a small band of Engineers. Because of this, the locks tended to be pretty much the same size, The "narrow" dimensions of 70ft x 7ft (21.4m x 2.1m) standard in England were eschewed for around 65ft by 9ft (19.8m x 2.7m). Slight variations were recorded, but only the Swansea at 69ft x 7ft 6ins (20.9m x 2.25m) was radically different.

Another major difference in canals either side of the border was that English canals generally formed an interconnected network; a spider's web of lines criss-crossing the country. Apart from the far-flung outposts, it was possible to reach most parts of the country. In Wales, physical constraints imposed by the terrain saw almost all canals use a valley and head for the sea, there to discharge cargo into ships for onward transmission. The only exception to this situation was the Tennant Canal – see Chapter Seven.

Most of these great enterprises made a good profit for their proprietors. Many were local industrialists who were two-way winners. With the availability of transport, they saw business profitability burgeoning. Adding to that gain was the money they made from their canal investment. Some dividends were amazing. On more than one occasion, the Swansea Canal paid a huge 14% to shareholders.

But, as in life everywhere, there were also losers. Investors in other canals lost their shirts when unexpected construction problems creating delays were compounded by the arrival of railways. Southern investors generally came out well; Midlands and North, less so. Neither the Ellesmere nor the Montgmeryshire ever made their investors rich.

The canals were dug by a very special breed of men. They gave us the term "navvy". The word was an abbreviation for "navigators", their "job description". They were a rough breed, mainly itinerants, who followed new canal construction around the country. Contemporary records often show them to be Irish, well inclined to spend their weekly earnings on strong liquor and to submit local communities, through which they dug, to reigns of terror for the duration.

At this distance, it is almost impossible to grasp just how much of a quantum leap forward the canals were. Take a small ironworks close to the head of the Glamorganshire Canal at Merthyr Tydfil. To reach Cardiff docks, a pack horse, carrying around 300lbs (150kg), would take well over three days to reach his destination. A cart with two horses would move something over a ton, but could take five days or more on the journey, provided the road wasn't too boggy.

A canal boat would carry nearly thirty tonnes, replacing over two hundred horses and drivers or twenty five carts, and complete the journey in under two days. To comprehend the scale of this change, a comparable improvement to today's transport system would need a device that could move a six thousand tonne load en bloc from Cardiff to Swansea in eight minutes.

The early and mid nineteenth century were the heyday for all concerned in this great transport development. But dark clouds were gathering in the shape of railways. Faster, more convenient and adaptable, and capable of carrying a greatly increased weight, the collieries and ironworks of south Wales were soon clamouring for their own private linking iron road. And those calls were heeded.

By the middle of that century, canal trade was haemorrhaging to the railways. Concerned for their investment, the proprietors tried to fight back, but were never going to be able to compete. Several, including most of the biggest ones, sold out to the Great Western Railway. That company's version of tender loving care for canals was total neglect, unless there was any chance of trade being fed along them to a railway siding, there to be forwarded by rail.

Patterns of trade were also changing as smaller ironworks were starting to close. Sir Henry Bessemer had perfected his process for making steel, an altogether more durable product than iron. This tended to be produced in larger and more specialised plants and the old ironworks, like the transport systems built to serve them, became yesterday's technology.

Coal was still being produced in abundance but, again, as smaller mines were being worked out, newer, deeper and bigger ones were replacing them. Whenever possible, pit heads were built at the most convenient point for some form of rail connection in preference to tramroad and canals. This was for mutual gain.

And if the colliery shaft was too far away, a branch line would be built. To paraphrase the old proverb: if the [colliery] mountain couldn't get to [the railway] Mahomet, Mahomet would get to the mountain.

Amalgamation and closures were increasingly to become the lot of canal companies. By the end of the nineteenth century, the canal age was over. Trade lingered on here and there, but the heady days of profit and busy boats had gone. Slowly the lines fell into disrepair. Some were infilled, others retained as water courses. The lower section of the Glamorganshire lasted in service until the end of the last war and was to be the final chapter in the story of carriage by inland waterway in south Wales.

But, limited salvation was to hand. After the 1939-45 war, a few enlightened souls saw this great transport system falling into decay and started fighting to save it. The Inland Waterways Association was formed in 1946 and campaigned vigorously to retain canals both for trade – and for leisure, a use hardly considered in those days. Sadly, in Wales, much had already been irrevocably lost by then.

The Monmouthshire and Brecknock and Abergavenny, amalgamated in 1865 to become the Monmouthshire and Brecon, still had long lengths in water and, running through the Brecon Beacons National Park, was a prime candidate for renewed leisure use. Today, this is achieved from south of Pontypool to Brecon and there are those who visualise a complete restoration one day.

Although other schemes to salvage lengths of canal, notably in the Neath area, proceed apace, the canal in south Wales, as a transport artery, is effectively dead. But that is not the end of the story.

Wherever man turned his ingenuity to building these waterways, there are relics and remains. Searching these out is not difficult and can provide endless fun, fascination and satisfaction for those who have the ability to create a greater mental picture from the limited features available to the eye.

Marvel at the resourcefulness displayed around every bend. These tortuous valleys provided a monumental challenge to engineers and labourers who had little more than picks and shovels with which to excavate; powered equipment was not an option in those days.

But above all, conjure up the image of a thriving, bustling transport artery, one that made the country what it is today. Without navigable inland waterways, the industrial and social development of Wales would have been radically different.

2. The Engineers

A small group of Engineers was responsible for pretty well the whole southern Welsh inland waterway system. Father of them – in more ways than one – was Thomas Dadford Senior.

His early life is obscure, but he seems to have originated in Worcestershire and is first recorded as working as assistant to the original canal engineer, James Brindley, on the Staffordshire and Worcestershire canal.

He was brought to Wales as Engineer for the first major canal: the Glamorganshire. His reputation at the time was a little tarnished. He had been engaged – with other famous engineers – on several canal projects around the country. Some of these had met with very limited success, indeed, he had been dismissed from the Dudley Canal extension project in the west Midlands.

Welsh air seemed to suit Dadford. Once here, he seldom strayed over the border again looking for work. Anxious to profit from both ends, he invariably took shares in the project which engaged him and, very unusually, owned the company who contracted for the construction.

His son was equally involved with south Wales. In addition to helping his father, he masterminded some of the projects alone. He had a brother – John – who was also in the same field. His major achievement was on the Montgomeryshire where he worked from 1794 to 1797. Then, with things getting on top of him to the extent that Thomas Jnr., had to help, he emigrated to the USA. Thomas Snr., was then summoned to assist.

As if this display of nepotism was not enough for Wales, Dadford Senior's long-time associate, Thomas Sheasby, arrived to work on these canals in 1791, adding his son to the list: yet another Thomas!

George Overton is another name indelibly associated with Welsh canals. He was a shareholder in the Hirwaun ironworks at the head of the Cynon Valley and was instrumental in the construction of many tramroads in the area, including the Penydarren – see Chapter Three. He was appointed Engineer for the Aberdare Canal, later working on improvements to the Glamorganshire.

William Kirkhouse came from Geordie stock, but was born and bred in the valleys. Little is known of his life other than that his employment was as a mining engineer. The skills learnt there clearly stood him in good stead when he masterminded the Tennant Canal.

But the most famous name on the roll call of canal engineers was undoubtably Thomas Telford. A Scot, born in 1757, he was trained as a stonemason. In 1782, he moved to London and worked for one William Poulteney. Much impressed by his work and knowledge, Poulteney gave Telford several commissions at which he was able to shine. One of these was re-modelling his castle at Shrewsbury.

His presence in the area coincided – in 1788 – with a vacancy for county surveyor. By now, his star was really in the ascendency. He was appointed part time to the Ellesmere Canal and full time after the then incumbent, Josiah Clowes, died.

Not that "full time" excluded him from anything else. His experience with road bridges and now a canal made him a very hot property. But he was still associated with the Ellesmere when the time came to cross the Dee valley at Pontcysyllte. The iron aqueduct stands memorial to his achievement. Sadly, the Ellesmere was his only canal work in Wales.

The doyen of west country engineers appeared briefly in Wales. James Green was born in Birmingham in 1781. His father was an engineer from which source he received his basic grounding. At the age of 20 he went to work for John Rennie. At that time, Rennie was reaching the end of his work on the Lancaster Canal, and was engrossed in construction of the Kennet and Avon. Although there is no proof, it seems almost certain that Green must have worked with him on this and other projects as his experience broadened.

He was sent to Devon by Rennie in 1806 and was soon undertaking work on his own account. This mainly involved land reclamation. He clearly found the Devonian pace of life to his liking because Green settled near Exeter in 1808, having been offered the post of Bridge Surveyor to the county. He carried out that work so effectively that there are still many main roads in Devon today that cross rivers on a Green bridge.

His first solo canal effort was at Bude. Once that project was under way, he spent some time reconstructing and widening the Exeter Canal. Subsequently, Green worked on the proposals to link the Bude Canal with the River Tamar to the south. It was already clear from his work that locks were anathema to him. As the Bude Canal progressed he came across ideas from an American, Robert Fulton, for water-powered inclined planes, and brought that theory of power into practice.

He continued to work the Devonshire bridges, but also found time to make proposals for The Liskeard and Looe Canal, which were not adopted, and the Rolle Canal at Torrington, which were. His election to the newly founded Institute of Civil Engineers (President Thomas Telford) was ratified in 1824, and seemed to confirm his status as a man going places.

By the 1830s, his work was in demand in Somerset with the Grand Western and Chard Canals, both tub boat size. Some lack of success here, again associated with his inclined planes, saw him leave both projects. Further failure was to follow in south Wales where the Kidwelly and Llanelli Canal, again with inclined planes, went way over budget and he was dismissed. His work in Cardiff with Bute Docks didn't involve inclined planes, and appeared to be much more successful.

After Wales, Green's canal building days were over. He moved to London and died there on February 13th 1849 aged 68.

There were several other lesser lights involved on the periphery of Welsh canal construction, but the foregoing were the main players. That so much of their work remains today is elegant testimony to their skills. May we expect to see today's transport infrastructure still functioning as intended at the end of the twenty second century? There is as much chance of that as there is of this writer being around to report the fact.

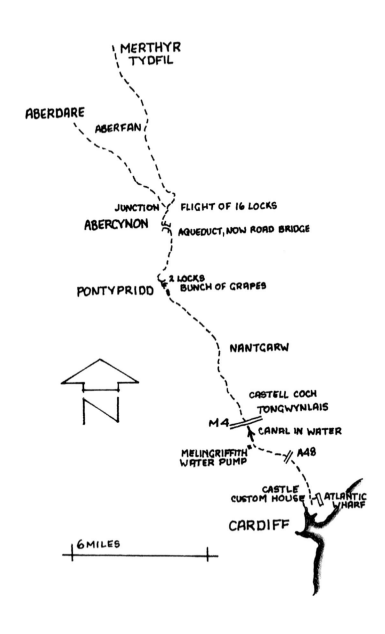

MERTHYR TYDFIL

ABERDARE

ABERFAN

JUNCTION — FLIGHT OF 16 LOCKS
ABERCYNON
AQUEDUCT, NOW ROAD BRIDGE

PONTYPRIDD — 2 LOCKS
BUNCH OF GRAPES

NANTGARW

CASTELL COCH
TONGWYNLAIS
M4 — CANAL IN WATER

MELINGRIFFITH
WATER PUMP — A48

CASTLE
CUSTOM HOUSE — ATLANTIC WHARF
CARDIFF

6 MILES

N

3. The Glamorganshire Canal

Then ...

Richard Crawshay, ironmaster of Merthy Tydfil, was the prime mover and biggest shareholder in this, the first major canal in Wales. And what a copper-bottomed investment it proved to be. Frantically busy for years, Crawshay and his successors were to benefit from regular canal profits and by seeing his business interests mushrooming because of access to cheap reliable transport.

An Act of Parliament was obtained in 1790. Thomas Dadford with his son Thomas Junior and Thomas Sheasby, were appointed to build the 24½ mile (39.5km) long canal from the Old Quay on the river Taff

Remains of the Glamorganshire Canal and an old bridge amidst the new development of Atlantic Wharf.

to Merthyr. This would need 49 locks, lifting the canal to 543ft (165.5m) above sea level, together with one short (115 yards/105m) tunnel near Cardiff Castle. For this, the consortium would be paid £48,000. The locks were to accommodate boats of 60ft x 8ft 6ins (18.2m x 2.5m), which would carry up to 25 tonnes.

Work started from the Merthyr end in August 1790 and proceeded apace. By 1792, construction was complete almost to Pontypridd and the size of the basin at Cardiff was settled. A short extension at the Merthyr end and several other small improvements were authorised, for which the contractors were looking for over £20,000 extra payment. Thomas Jnr. meanwhile had left the Glamorganshire to work on the Leominster and, later, the Monmouthshire canal.

On February 10th 1794, to great celebration, the first boat arrived in Cardiff from Merthyr. The canal was a living entity. Now, the iron capital of the world – Merthyr – had the transport it needed to service its ever increasing output. A twenty hour journey, and the product would be alongside a ship.

But recriminations were soon to start flying thick and fast. Acrimony would be the byword for this canal, its directors, shareholders, users and neighbours. As ever, the legal jackals found rich pickings

The total bill for canal, extensions, and basin at Cardiff turned out to be £103,600. In December 1794, the canal breached. The contractors – still Dadford Snr. and Sheasby – who were continuing to manage the canal, wanted payment up-front before repairing it. The company refused. Piqued, the contractors withdrew their men. The owners alleged a previous overpayment of £17,000. Dadford and Sheasby were arrested.

An arbitrator, Robert Whitworth, another eminent canal engineer, was appointed to consider the case. He decided the sum overpaid was just £1,500.

A new Engineer, Patrick Copeland, was designated and subsequent quarrels – very bitter in some cases – were confined to the boardroom. Richard Crawshay seems to have been quite an aggressive businessman, even by the standards of those days. He was accused of pressurising boatowners to carry for him before anyone else. Disaffected shareholders even went to the length of building a separate tramway from Merthyr to Abercynon, the Penydarren Tramroad.

Battles over the limited water supply in the valley were to continue intermittently for over thirty years. The company were forced to build new reservoirs and back-pumping was installed in an attempt to provide sufficient water for the levels of boat activity.

But all these problems made little impact on the profits. Trade flourished. There was even an *embarras de richesses* as bank balances mushroomed. This created something of a problem, as, by the company's constitution, dividends were limited to 8%.

By 1806, the board of directors resolved to return 20% of the tolls that traders had paid. That satisfied only a proportion of users. In this acrimonious atmosphere, some wanted permanently reduced tolls and applied to local magistrates for an order. This was granted for the financial years 1808 and 1809. Six years later, with money accumulating

Glamorganshire Canal remains under Kingsway, Cardiff.

again, the directors decided to reduce charges by 10%.

This had an altogether negative result in that profits actually increased because of the extra traffic generated. It was then decided to suspend tolls for the last quarter of the financial year. This was continued into the first quarter of the next year. Subsequently, large sums were returned to carriers into the 1820s.

The sheer size of these profits indicates that trade was booming. Cardiff docks just could not cope, and the volume of boat movements created a

Abercynon

downward water current that saw boats bringing imported iron ore up to Merthyr unable to load more than about 15 tonnes. Beyond that, the horses could not move their load.

Congestion in Cardiff was such that the company decided to improve the dock. The original area had been enlarged in 1798 by building a sea lock down the Taff river. This had the effect of allowing vessels of up to 200 tonnes access to the quays. By 1821, an engineer, George Overton, was appointed to suggest methods of improvement. His report concluded that the canal be widened and deepened from the sea lock back to Cardiff where a new basin should be built.

It was also time for more conflict, this time from two implacable foes. One, Richard Blakemore, ran a works at Melingriffith. He had been in dispute with the company over water supplies, and was the cause of an undershot waterwheel pump being installed there in 1807. In 1824, he obtained an injunction to stop the company increasing the depth of the basin in Cardiff on the grounds that it would adversely affect his water supply.

The other opposition came from the Marquess of Bute. He was against further water extraction because it might affect the local fishery. That this was an early demonstration of conservation at work is doubtful: it probably had more to do with thoughts that his way to increased riches was to built a harbour himself. James Green was employed to draw up proposals.

An Act was obtained in 1830 to build a ship canal, but the work was never effected. The company, frustrated by the Marquess, were stuck. They had no land on which to build, and things were getting desperate.

By 1830 over 200,000 tonnes of cargo moved along the canal. Steam coal was now adding to the tonnage and Sunday working had been introduced, followed by the installation of lighting in 1833 to allow traffic day and night. To this end, extra staff were appointed to give 24 hour cover.

Meanwhile, the noble lord had plans drawn for a new dock. This eventually became West Bute Dock and opened in 1839 with a new link to the canal. Now, trade had reached almost 350,000 tonnes p.a. The canal just could not cope with this volume of boat movements and water became an increasingly scarce commodity. There were well over 200 boats at work, and the canal was approaching its maximum capacity.

Interesting experiments meanwhile were taking place on the Penydarren Tramway. Steam locomotives from the hand of that Cornish engineering genius Richard Trevithick were tried, but with only limited success. They were short of power to carry freight uphill. Not in any way daunted, proposals were made in 1834 for a full railway between Merthyr and Cardiff. Isambard Kingdom Brunel was consulted about the possibility and an Act was granted in 1836.

Descendants of Richard Crawshay still ran the Glamorganshire, with much the same degree of confrontation, the truculent gene in his makeup having been handed down the line. The names appearing in early records of the Taff Vale Railway Company were many of those who had originally quarrelled with Crawshay and built the tramroad; thus were the battle lines drawn almost half a century later.

The interloper reached Abercynon by October 1840, Merthyr six months later. The war was on. Initially, the canal held its own; there was more than enough trade for all. Then, William Crawshay II, the canal company chairman, made a fatal error.

THE OLD CUSTOM HOUSE
1821-98

WITH THE COMPLETION OF THE GLAMORGANSHIRE CANAL
IN 1798, THE MARITIME COMMERCIAL CENTRE MOVED
FROM THE TOWN RIVER QUAY TO THE CANAL WHARF IN
THIS VICINITY, RESULTING IN THE TRANSFER OF THE 18th
CENTURY CUSTOM HOUSE FROM ST. MARY STREET TO
THIS BUILDING AT THE EAST WHARF. IT WAS ERECTED
IN 1821 AND LATER EXTENDED, BUT BECAME
PROGRESSIVELY ISOLATED WITH THE RISE OF THE
BUTE DOCKS FROM 1839 ONWARDS. IN 1898 IT WAS
REPLACED BY THE THIRD CUSTOM HOUSE AT THE
PIER HEAD END OF BUTE STREET.

THE BUILDING WAS ACQUIRED AND RESTORED
FOR ITS OWN USE BY THE LAND AUTHORITY
FOR WALES AND FORMALLY RE-OPENED BY
THE SECRETARY OF STATE FOR WALES IN
MAY 1986

17

DONATED BY FORMER CITY COUNCILLOR T.H. ROCHE, J.P. OCT 1989

*The Old Custom House in Cardiff is on Custom
House Street. This plaque records its history.*

There had been muttering amongst those concerned that an amalgamation of dock, canal and railway would create an exceedingly profitable concern for all. By 1844, the deal was on. Without warning, Crawshay suddenly demanded compensation. The rest looked askance and the arrangement fell apart. The noble lord agreed with the railway that they would bring their trade through the port at reduced rates, rather than go elsewhere.

With that move, the canal's fate was sealed. As coal traffic burgeoned, another dock was built at East Bute and opened in 1859, a canal link being provided. But waterborne tonnage levels were falling away dramatically as the railway encroached further, building connections to canalside collieries and ironworks.

An attempt to buy the canal by the Bute Trustees in 1866 was rebuffed. Ten years later, the 8% dividend was paid for the last time. In 1883 the Marquess of Bute made an offer to buy all the canal shares. This was finally accepted, with the Crawshays seeing the writing on the wall and not liking the spelling. As chairman, the Marquess asked for a report on the navigation. It was in a very poor state of repair.

In 1897, the canal and dock operations were combined and the name changed to The Cardiff Railway Company. The section from Abercynon to Merthyr became disused by 1898, and by 1913 no boats moved above Pontypridd. It needed a breach at Nantgarw in 1942 before the last rites were finally said over this wonderful money-making line, the local council buying the canal and obtaining a Closure Act.

But one last breath was drawn. The Sea Lock pound continued in use until after the war before it too succumbed.

And Now ...

For a canal so recently closed, there is remarkably little remaining. That inevitable killer of old canal lines – roads – has reaped a heavy toll hereabouts. But there are still some fascinating bits waiting to be discovered by the assiduous seeker. From Cardiff to Abercynon, they are few and completely unconnected. From Abercynon north, there is enough to make a walk.

In Cardiff, West Bute Dock now masquerades under a rather grander title: Atlantic Wharf. This has become part of the multi-million clear-up operation in the old docks area. Gone is trade; tourists and town houses are now the vogue.

A few yards of the old canal linking into West Bute Docks will be found at ST 191758 on Schooner Way, a delightful mix of ancient and modern. Then the canal has gone, but its memory lingers. Custom House Square, close to the main train station, is where the customs house was located. The building is still there. East Canal Wharf, West Canal Wharf and Canal Parade are all in the same area and permanent reminders of what once was.

An old canal bridge is now used as a pedestrian underpass at Kingsway, in the centre of Cardiff, just outside the east wall of Cardiff Castle at ST 183766. The elegant curves associated with canal bridge construction are very evident here.

From this point, the line of the canal effectively ceases to exist until a fascinating recreation of the Melingriffith water pump. Although classed as a rebuild, the amount of work carried out brings it very firmly into the "this-is-my-grandfather's-axe-although-I-fitted-a-new-shaft-and-my-father-fitted-a-new-head" category. It can be found on Tŷ-Mawr Road at ST 144803. An interpretation board there explains it all.

The machinery for weighing boats on the Glamorganshire Canal at Tongwynlais (see Chapter 13) was saved and re-located to the Waterway Museum at Stoke Bruern (Northants) where it is now on display.

A few yards north, a length of the canal has been retained in water as a Nature Trail. Just under a mile long and including the first example of a Glamorganshire lock, the section finishes against the side of a new road scheme connected with the M4 motorway (ST 136814). A huge Asda supermarket and a MacDonalds will be found by the road. There is a section beyond this road, although it is but a muddy trickle.

To Pontypridd now, probably driving along the very road that destroyed the canal's course. Take the left turn into the town, noting that on the right, across the road, is the factory of Brown Lenox and Co Ltd. The canal is just behind this building. Through the town and back over the river is Ynysangharad Road. Here, behind the Bunch of Grapes pub (ST 078902) is a two chamber staircase lock.

A right turn will take you along a path that was the course of the canal, whilst turning left leads alongside a genuine bit of canal in water. Around the back of Brown Lenox's works – which is only a footpath – and into another section which is clearly canal. This ends where the new road has cut away the surrounding landscape, some 400 yards (365m) along.

An old colliery site on the southern edge of Abercynon, closed in 1988, has now become Navigation Park (ST 082944). Close by, near the railway overbridge and the fire station, is Navigation House. This is where the Penydarren tramroad reached the canal. Its course is signposted and the Taff Trail (a walking/cycling route from Cardiff to Brecon) uses some of the route. A plaque marking the operation of this early tramroad will be found just outside the fire station.

Look also at the bridge over the river. This was originally a canal aqueduct before improvement and extension saw the road use it as well. This spot is at the foot of Cefn Glas where the canal climbed over 200 ft (61m) by the sixteen Abercynon Locks. These were grouped into – and universally known as – "the eleven" and "the five". Under the railway, there is a footpath leading up the hill between houses, alongside a church and behind Lock Street.

Halfway up, the Aberdare Canal left in a westerly direction – see Chapter Nine. A house in Springfield Drive, just above the site of the junction has part of an old lock chamber almost forming a glorified rockery, but also giving the line of the canal. The roadside sign "Dock Cottages" helps locate the actual junction. Here the GCC maintenance yard was located. A description of activities at this busy location follows.

From Abercynon, the easiest way to access the various canal remains is by walking the Taff Trail as far as Merthyr. As previously mentioned, this uses the Penydarren Tramroad at the lower side of Abercynon. Close to the new A470 at ST 088962, Cefnglas Lock, number 9, was located. You reach this along a byroad off the A4054 at ST 096966; the main road has no exit to here. After crossing the Taff on a splendid single arched bridge, the canal course can be seen. A bridge still exists at Pont-y-Dderwen, a little to the right.

From here, much of the old towing path is used by the Trail. High on the valley side, it must have been a dramatic place to see canal boats working. The straggling ill-fated village of Aberfan soon appears, much of it below canal level.

Reconstructed pump at Melingriffith on the Glamorganshire Canal. Water was raised from Taff to canal by the water-wheel.

It was on a rainy Friday morning, October 21st 1966, that a huge colliery spoil heap above the town avalanched down the hill (SO 070004) covering the place in thick slimy black mud. Houses and the village school were engulfed and 144 people, mainly junior school children, perished in the morass.

The canal passes close to the cemetery where the remains of those victims are interred (SO 070000). A corner of the graveyard, high on the hill, is set aside for them, each with identical memorials. To see the graves is to appreciate again the scale of the tragedy. Even more poignant is the fact that several of the children have now been joined there by their parents. Further along the towing path is the actual site of the disaster at Moy Road. A Garden of Remembrance has been created, just below the level of the canal.

Collieries were sited all along this side of the valley. At Troedyrhiw, there were two – Furnace and Castle – and the typical cottages associated with mining here back onto the canal.

Abercanaid was another mining village; now it's just a village. The canal skirts to the west of the place, passing the site of two collieries. The giant Hoover electrical firm is located here, still surviving despite taking a fearful bashing in the early 1990s. Having offered free airline tickets for purchasers of their products, they were overwhelmed by applications. It cost the company millions of pounds to meet their commitments and the jobs of those who floated the scheme.

One somewhat tenuous link with the world of entertainment far removed from these Welsh valleys is provided by Petula Clarke, the singer. She progressed through child prodigy to recording artist, mother and international entertainer, but her family roots were in this village. Her grandparents lived here and she holidayed with them regularly during the 1939-45 war years.

The canal is just traceable for another half mile or so before disappearing under a mass of roadworks. From here, turn left and walk to the train station in Merthyr Tydfil for return transport.

Maps

Geographers *A to Z Street Atlas of Cardiff and Newport* shows some of the canal's course through Cardiff and is invaluable in locating the canal in Pontypridd. Ordnance Survey Sheets 161, 170 and 171 cover the whole course of the canal.

The machinery for weighing boats on the Glamorganshire Canal at Tongwynlais (see Chapter 13) was saved and re-located to the Waterway Museum at Stoke Bruerne (Northants) where it is now on display.

Public Transport

Regional Railways' Cardiff to Merthyr Tydfil service follows some of the canal's route, and bus services radiate from both Cardiff and Merthyr Tydfil.

As it (perhaps) was

*This story graced the pages of **Waterways World** magazine in March 1991, part of the research for a book, **Merthyr Boat Boy** by Clive Thomas, Gill Foley & Josephine Jeremiah. This section ([c] J. Jeremiah) is reproduced with her kind permission which is gratefully acknowledged. It's a vivid – if fictional – re-creation of life afloat a century and a half ago.*

Boat Boy On The Glamorganshire Canal

It was in 1841, the year I became twelve, that I started working for my father as a boat boy on the Glamorganshire Canal. My father had bought his own boat and carried all manner of goods up and down the waterway. He was a "hobbler" or bye-trader which meant that he could trade independently of the Canal Company.

I had heard all about the canal before, of course, how it joined the towns of Merthyr and Cardiff and how, although the distance was only 24½ miles, there were many locks before it reached the sea. Yet I had never made the journey along even half its length.

When we left our house in Merthyr that morning my mother gave us a bundle of food as we would be away from home for some days on the trip to Cardiff and back. Waving goodbye, I walked proudly alongside my father. I felt a different person. Was this really me, David Thomas, about to go down the Glamorganshire Canal to the sea?

My first task was to collect our horse, Siencyn, from the stables whilst my father checked the cargo of iron bars in our boat. The horse whinnied with pleasure at seeing me and a feeling of happiness coursed through me as I rubbed his nose, put on his harness and led him out into the sunlight.

Siencyn and I made our way to the boat which had been moored overnight near the Ynysfach ironworks, already loaded. Then, when all was ready, we proceeded to Parliament Lock, which was adjacent to the works.

A boat had just come up the lock and the boat boy had left the gate open for us. I led Siencyn to the lockside and my father steered the boat into the lock. I shut the lock gate and went forward to open one of the lower paddles with my windlass to release the water. On the far side of the lock, the lock-keeper opened the other paddle and slowly the boat began to go down in the lock. He was pleased to see me and asked me how I was enjoying my first day at work. I replied that it suited me fine. The lock-keeper knew me well, we had chatted many times before, but as I went further down the canal I found out that everybody seemed to know everybody else's business.

Passing the cottages at Rhyd y Car, my father guided the boat along, whilst I led Siencyn along the towpath. A double lock stood on a gentle curve of the canal at Glyndyrys. Behind the lock house was a large reservoir which had been built to store water in times of drought, when low water frequently caused problems for the canal traffic.

Once through the locks, we made our way past Quay Row to Abercanaid where I saw the substantial dock which was used for the loading and unloading of goods and raw materials for the Plymouth ironworks. That day the wharf was a hive of industry.

Moving onwards past Pond Row and Graig Cottages, I saw the workings of Graig Pit where women and children worked as well as men. I could see barefoot girls, black with dust, carrying baskets of coal upon their heads. I thought then of the little children working underground in this mine, looking after the airdoors or pushing the trams, hardly ever seeing the sunshine.

Even though the marks of industry were apparent along the canal the signs of late spring were everywhere, too. I listened in vain for the song of the nightingale as we went by the inn at Llwyn yr Eos, a favourite mooring place for boatmen, but the air was full of the sound of other birdsong and that morning the canal had been frequented by pied wagtails, robins and song thrushes, to name but a few.

After Abercanaid the canal took us out into the countryside which was a welcome relief after the hustle and bustle of the town and its surroundings. The hillsides on either side of the canal were wooded and this lock-free stretch had conspicuous clumps of those flowers called yellow flags. We worked easily through the locks at Perth y Gleision and Ty'n y Cae and there was no waiting for us again for, as a boat came up out of the lock, so we went in. My father assured me that it was not always as easy as that. Sometimes, when traffic was heavy the waiting could be long and tedious.

It is not the way of things always to run smoothly. When we reached Pont y Dderwen I noticed that Siencyn was limping slightly so we stopped near the bridge for me to inspect his hooves for stones. Luckily I found out what was causing the trouble. Looking over the valley from this point, I could see a stagecoach on the turnpike road. It appeared incredibly small from that distance. I could also see that the final touches were being put to the Taff Vale Railway.

Whilst he was waiting for me to deal with the horse, my father had struck up a conversation with a farmer. They were talking about the new railway development in the valley below and both were of the opinion that it would not be successful and that there was no cause for concern. He was by no means persuaded that the new railway could herald the beginning of the end for the canal. In the event he was to be proved wrong, but that came much later.

Meanwhile there was hard work to do as we brought the boat through the flight of locks above Navigation. Here was an impressive piece of engineering work, a concentration of sixteen locks in a distance of one mile, one of the locks being the deepest in the world at 14ft 6in.

This section was also a heavily congested part of the canal as it was standard practice to save water by working turns. Boats were passed alternatively upwards and downwards through the locks, making each lockful of water pass two boats. The system, though irksome in the extreme, made a real saving, especially in times of low water, as each lockful meant about 56,000 gallons of water. It was to everyone's advantage to save water but a great nuisance to have to wait a long time at every lock.

By the time we reached the junction with the Aberdare Canal my father decided to moor for the night in the winding hole above Lock y Waun. It was still early but as it was my first day at work my father thought we would pay a visit to my brother, William, who worked for the Canal Company and who lived nearby. We were persuaded to stay the night at my brother's house and Bethan, William's wife, cooked us a savoury supper over the fire. I had not realised just how dog-tired I was and after supper I mumbled my thanks and staggered off to bed. Once there I fell into a dreamless sleep and did not wake again until morning.

There was a very early start the next morning to make up for lost time. After all the hard work of yesterday every bone in my body ached from the unaccustomed activity and I just wanted to turn over and go back to sleep, but Bethan shook me and I stumbled to my feet. William and my father were already outside, and, after hastily chewing on a crust of bread, I joined them. In contrast to the bright morning of the previous day there was now a light drizzle falling. My father handed me a piece of sacking to drape around my shoulders to keep out the worst of the wet. Then I went under the foredeck where Siencyn's fodder was kept. He was eagerly awaiting his morning feed and was soon munching away contentedly.

I looked at our boat and was pleased with what I saw. It was a serviceable craft, not beautiful perhaps, but strong and sturdy, measuring 60ft long and 8ft 6in wide. Pointed at both ends, there was a cabin at the stern with a berth along each side and a stove at one end of it. The chimney was cut down to roof level because the bridges were low. Our boat was decorated with red lozenges and crescents at the bow and stern and there was a "four pears" design on the cabin sides.

As I was contemplating the scene with satisfaction my father called out to me to wake up and get a move on, otherwise the world and his wife would be down at Navigation before us. I jumped to it as I was eager to see the place, never having been there before. First we had to negotiate the rest of the flight of locks and cross the stone aqueduct over the river Taff. On our left was the canal basin where the Penydarren Tramway ended and straight ahead was Navigation House where the Canal Company's business was transacted. There were spacious wharves at Navigation and the company's maintenance yard, sawpit and drydock were all situated here. It was also an important boat building centre for the canal.

The waterway now curved around to the right, widening below Navigation, then narrowing again as we made our way back into the countryside. To the left of us was Craig Evan Leyshon Common and to the right the river Taff meandered its way alongside the canal. At the end of the common was Ynyscaedudwg Lock and then we entered a pleasantly wooded stretch of canal along Bedwenarth Wood. Now the air was filled with the scent of bluebells, indeed the woods were carpeted with them. The drizzle had lessened and the sunlight began to filter through the trees. It felt good to be alive walking along the towpath with Siencyn.

I began to notice the sound made by the water voles as they dived underwater at the approach of our boat. The moorhens, those secretive nervous birds, looked so comical with their red and yellow beaks and there was no end of panicking when our boat came too near. Once I saw a snake, swimming with its head held high out of the water, and another time a stoat ran across the top of a pair of lock gates right in front of me, as bold as could be. Yes, I was certainly lucky to be in this position, far luckier than some of the boat boys I had met coming up the flight, who were not working for their fathers. It was common for children at work in those days to be ill-treated; few people thought much about it, it was the way of the world.

Several more locks were worked before reaching the Newbridge Chainworks, right next to the canal at Pontypridd. A number of boats were moored in the upper works basin, above the two Ynysangharad locks, waiting to discharge their cargoes of iron bars, but the way through the locks was clear for us.

Soon we were passing the village of Nantgarw and the canal-side, bottle-shaped kilns of the Nantgarw Pottery, once the producer of world famous porcelain, now manufacturing earthenware. My father had a clay pipe from these works, the bowl decorated with oak leaves. Boats often moored up at Nantgarw for the night as it was here that many boatmen lived. It was convenient for them to leave their boats near the village and walk to their homes where they would spend the night. Usually a single journey up or down the waterway took two days, so it was to their advantage that their homes were situated mid-way along the canal.

The valley narrows after Nantgarw and shortly we came to the great Treble Locks. It was an exciting experience for me to see a staircase of three locks like this. They were built next to each other with no canal pound in between, so that the gates between one lock and the next appeared to be quite tall. Each of the locks had a fall of 14ft so when boats were deep in the lock the gates would tower above them. Working through a staircase of locks raised problems. Once a boat was in the staircase, no boat could move the opposite way in these locks until the first one had cleared them all. I think that out of all the congestion on the canal it was the worst at Treble Locks, where working turns was again the normal practice. Luck was with us that day, however, for the hold-up was only slight compared with that of yesterday.

As we left the locks the valley widened out again, but in the distance I could see the hills closing in once more, leaving only a narrow gap with wooded slopes on either side of the gorge. Then we passed through three more locks at Taff's Well, Cae Glas and Portobello before reaching Tongwynlais Lock.

Our boat going down the canal carried a load of about twenty-four tons. In short water times this would fall to around eighteen to twenty tons. The boats coming up the canal, however, only carried fifteen to eighteen tons. The reason for this was that the constant working of the locks caused a downward current which made it difficult for a horse to pull as heavy a boat upstream as he could downstream.

While we were waiting to go through Tongwynlais Lock I saw a loaded boat go into another lock alongside. This was a special lock over which a gigantic weighing machine was suspended. I watched the water being drained out of the lock and the boat coming to rest on the pan of the machine. My father told me that, as the unladen weight of each boat on the canal was already known, the weight of the cargo could be calculated and a toll charged for it. The toll of the Glamorganshire Canal Company was 2d a ton per mile for coal, limestone, iron ore, manure, bricks, clay and sand, and 5d a ton per mile for iron, timber goods and merchandise. On this occasion our boat was not weighed as the weighing machine was not used every time each boat passed through Tongwynlais Lock. It would have caused far too much delay. When our turn came, we passed through Tongwynlais, leaving the hills behind.

All along the canal, flowering plants were beginning to bloom. Here were blue water forget-me-nots, yellow marsh marigolds and the white spears of arrowheads. I could also smell the wild garlic which grew most abundantly along this stretch. The alder trees and willows were overhanging the canal, and now and then I caught a glimpse of a kingfisher, just a quick flash of blue, flying a few feet above the canal, always in front.

As the day wore on we began to get near to Cardiff and a feeling of excitement rose within me. I had never seen the sea and I was longing to know what it looked like. Yet there were more sights to enjoy before we reached our journey's end. Near Melingriffith Lock there was a water pump operated by a large water wheel. This raised water into the canal and had been built as a result of a dispute between the Canal Company and the nearby Melingriffith Tinplate Works.

Then we passed through four more locks before reaching North Road Lock in Cardiff where there was a low, thatched cottage with white-washed walls. An interesting cast iron bridge was below the lock and then the canal curved around in the shadow of the castle wall. Soon we came to Crockherbtown Lock. Immediately below this lock was the entrance to the only tunnel on the canal. The tunnel was 115 yards long and it was my job to lead Siencyn up a paved horse way to street level and across the top of the tunnel. Meanwhile my father manhandled the boat through by grasping the chain fixed to the tunnel wall.

On leaving the tunnel, the canal followed the course of the old town wall and was hemmed in by row upon row of houses. In a little while we were entering the canal basin where our cargo of iron was to be unloaded. I had reached the end of my journey down the Glamorganshire Canal.

I will never forget my first sight of those busy crowded wharves, the ships with their tall masts, the raucous crying of the seagulls, the smell of the tarred ropes and of the sea itself; the sea upon which ships took iron from Merthyr to the four corners of the earth.

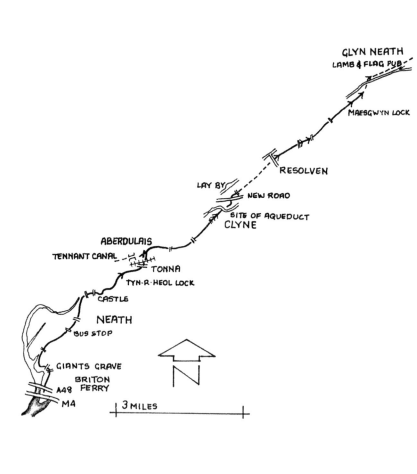

GLYN NEATH
LAMB & FLAG PUB
MAESGWYN LOCK
RESOLVEN
LAY BY
NEW ROAD
SITE OF AQUEDUCT
CLYNE
ABERDULAIS
TENNANT CANAL
TONNA
TYN·R·HEOL LOCK
CASTLE
NEATH
BUS STOP
GIANTS GRAVE
BRITON FERRY
A48
M4

N

3 MILES

4. The Neath Canal

Then ...

Canals in the Neath area owed much to Lord Vernon, although there had been several efforts at constructing artificial navigations based on the river Neath prior to his interest. The river had been made navigable to Neath, and when a short artificial cut with locks was built, Aberdulais could be reached.

The motivation behind this canal project was slightly different to the Glamorganshire – examined in Chapter Three. This time, the need was to transport iron ore and coal from producing to manufacturing areas around Neath Abbey which already had access to ships.

Maesgwyn, on the restored section of the Neath Canal.

As originally planned, the canal would start at Glynneath and head towards Neath Abbey, ten miles (16.1km) to the south west. There would be nineteen locks, nominally 60 feet by 8ft 10ins (16.2 x 2.65m). Sections of the river were to be canalised according to the original proposal by Thomas Dadford Jnr., but these were eventually abandoned in favour of an artificial waterway for the whole length.

The Act was granted in 1791 and construction began. Dadford was in charge, with one Jonathan Gee as contractor. Building north from Neath, progress was swift and Dadford had reached Ynysbwllog where an aqueduct would take the canal from the east to the opposite side of the river valley. Here things ground to a halt, temporarily.

Dadford had by this time agreed to take on construction of the Monmouthshire Canal – see Chapter Five – and his replacement was Thomas Sheasby. He fell behind the agreed construction schedule and, in 1794, had not completed the work. As the directors met to consider the position, a novel excuse for ditching their errant contractor was presented to them. He was arrested – as noted in Chapter Three.

With work at a standstill, the company answer was a do-it-yourself one. They took over the work and the canal was opened the following year. The efficacy of their workmen was called into question for several years afterwards as complete locks needed rebuilding, and other "improvements" had to be undertaken.

But one small part, as detailed in the original Act, was never completed. A lock linking canal and river at Neath was soon perceived to be unnecessary as events conspired to change the original thinking.

On the coast, near where Briton Ferry now sprawls, was a spot known as Giant's Grave. Here, ships on the river Neath tied up to carry freight to an ironworks. Being able to use this facility attracted the Canal Company and in 1798 an Act was obtained for the 2½ mile (4km) extension southward from Neath.

Along the projected course, a small private canal already existed. This was the Penrhiwtyn Canal, built by Lord Vernon at the time the Neath was being constructed. This was just over a mile (1.8km) long, lock-free and linked Raby's ironworks with the pill at Giant's Grave. It

Resolven Lock, Neath Canal.

was bought by the Neath company and absorbed into the southern extension.

Now, the company had a good terminal for sea-going ships. To improve it even more, some basic dredging was done and flood gates built. Thus the work was complete, trade flowed in increasing quantities and returns to the investors showed a handsome profit.

But industry developed, and not only canalside. Beyond the head of navigation, there were demands for improved transport. Some, more far-seeing, wanted to link the Neath with the Glamorganshire Canal. Several options were considered. A turnpike road, tramroad, and canal all had their proponents.

In the event, the Aberdare Canal – see Chapter Nine – provided a navigable link from that town to the Glamorganshire at Abercynon, and tram roads would run from head of navigation, through Hirwaun where there was substantial industry, to Glynneath, there to link into the Neath Canal.

Before the Aberdare was finished, the Neath benefited by carrying a good level of trade originating from works alongside the tramroad. Once the former was opened in 1812, this flow of traffic was almost exclusively to the east rather than west to the Neath. This state of affairs was advanced by business failures in the Hirwaun area, and by 1820 the Neath to Abercynon link was severed.

Another tramroad headed northeast to Dinas. There, limestone and fireclay were won and transported to the head of navigation. Trade on this section endured for many years after the Aberdare link was severed.

One other small development at the south end of the canal was that Lord Vernon extended the canal around the pill to the south side, there to link with improved shipping facilities. In future years, this would be lengthened in stages by almost a mile (1.5km) to reach other developing foundries and steelworks.

1824 brought a radical change in the operation of the Neath Canal. It was on Thursday morning, May 13th that the Tennant Canal opened – see Chapter Seven. This gave the Neath canal traders access to much improved port facilities at Swansea, reducing considerably the traffic passing through Neath docks.

Railways did not arrive in the area until 1851, by which time trade on the canal was firmly established. Many of the collieries and ironworks were built alongside the canal and the railway could not reach them directly.

But as new enterprises opened, they were more attracted to the railways and by the mid 1870s, with older works and pits closing, the inevitable was under way. Already, the southern extensions had become disused as easier terrain had allowed the railways to make direct connections in the area.

In just a few short years, the previously bustling canal had become one of almost abandonment. The proprietors considered converting the line to a railway, but this idea came to naught.

By the turn of the century, traffic was almost gone and the canal's main function was that of a water supply channel. As with so many canals around the country, this ensured the integrity of the line into the leisure era.

Today, the canal is owned by shareholders, principally BP, who have accepted the overtures of the local preservation society and have agreed in principle to restoration throughout.

And Now ...

A WORD OF WARNING: The Neath Canal is privately owned and there is NO Right of Way along the towing path. However, access is freely allowed and there are no problems in walking.

Apart from a short section below Resolven, the line is more or less intact. This exploration will start at the southern end and work north.

Easiest point of access to the southern section is in Briton Ferry at the end of Church Street (SS 735944). Here a now flat bridge crosses the water as the A48 Earlswood Bypass soars overhead. Turn left and, by limbo-dancing under a road bridge not too far above the towing path, the end of the canal is reached.

This is just beyond a pretty stone bridge inside what is now an aggregate suppliers yard. Here was the area of the old quay where cargoes were trans-shipped. The furthest section has been infilled now. This was once Briton Ferry steelworks and, although closed for many years, it explains why the road overhead is so high.

When first mooted, the road, if it were to follow the course deemed most suitable by the planners, had to cross the works. Therefore, a good overhead clearance was needed. But the plans were sidelined for some years during which time the steelworks closed. Despite that, the bridge was still built to the originally planned height.

Return the way you came and continue along the towing path. This is industrial Wales at its untidiest with factories or derelict land on either side. The canal is cut into the craggy side of Warren Hill here for a short distance.

A swing to the right as the terrain flattens and the canal reaches a couple of lowered bridges at Giants Grave. Cross to the right hand side and continue the exploration. The next (stone) bridge is actually a roving bridge which allowed the towing path to change sides, but now the path stays on the right.

Shortly, the towing path becomes overgrown but a metalled road almost alongside serves the purpose very well. At the next bridge, an entrance to the council rubbish tip, cross and take the path to the left hand side of the water. Industry is still all around although the hills which will eventually turn this into a thoroughly dramatic canal can be seen in the distance.

A series of bridges follows. One, a pipe bridge is followed almost at once by a narrow stone one (SS 742962) which will give access to a return bus.

• Leave the canal, cross the railway, taking great care as high speed trains use this, and it is located on a bend. The return bus leaves from across the road in Penrhiwtyn.

On the outskirts of Neath, ancient industry crowds the canal giving something of a hemmed-in feeling. A flattened bridge on Canal Road (SS 749974) starts the canal around the edge of town. A series of bridges takes railway and roads over the water with the towing path unimpaired.

• Leave the canal at Bridge Street, turn right, cross the main road into Angel Street and follow this road to the bus station.

PLEASE NOTE: This next section will involve crossing sections where canal water runs over the towing path. Appropriate footwear is essential.

The castle at Neath sits on a hard mound by the canal and is an impressive ruin that has been partially restored. It dates from 1284.

Surprisingly quickly, Neath is behind and, apart from roads, the

Weed-cutting boat on the Neath Canal.

46

prospect ahead is one of unalloyed joy. Canal and river come very close together for a section and are intermittently close for the next half mile. The first lock – Tyn'r Heol – is soon reached, decayed but by no means irrevocably lost.

You may have noticed that the canal appears to have acquired a rusty hue. It has. This phenomenon is caused by water draining into the canal that has passed through deposits of iron ore. Particles of the ore are carried into the water, covering everything in an ochre tint. Similar effects can be seen on the English canal system at Kidsgrove on the Trent and Mersey, and Worsley near Manchester, on the Bridgewater Canal.

A spillway into the river crosses the towing path with only a brick midway for use as a stepping stone. The steeply rising hillside on the right has a good covering of trees and looks very imposing.

Another – more lengthy – spillway soon follows. Not as deep as the first one, there is still ample scope for wet feet by the more careless. At this point, the towing path is no more than a narrow isthmus between artificial and natural watercourses.

At the next road bridge, Tonna is reached. The Railway Tavern stands seventy five yards to the left. Beyond, under the railway, an elegant stone bridge takes the towing path over a canal junction on a skew. This is the start of the Tennant Canal – see Chapter Seven – at Aberdulais Junction (SS 774994).

The canal now follows a generally north westerly course up the Vale of Neath, sharing the available space with river and road. Sadly (for the peace of canal explorers) a new road is being thrown through the valley to relieve the overcrowded A465. This is close for the next mile and very close towards Clyne, passing two locks en route. At SN 802009 this section of the exploration must finish. A few hundred yards ahead stands Ynysbwllog aqueduct – just. This was already close to failure in 1979 when an exceptional flood in the river washed away the central span. There is no bar to walking to the limit should you so choose.

• From Clyne, a bus will return you to Neath.

Beyond the damaged aqueduct, re-alignment of the canal has taken place to accommodate the new road. Only a short section of canal exists currently. To access this means either travelling to Resolven and back down the A465, or back to Aberdulais and up the same road. A layby on that road at S0 804013 is almost opposite a Public Footpath through a farmyard. This leads to the towing path, but there is not much to walk. Incidentally, admire the British Longhorn cows in the fields here. These are prize beasts, lovingly cared for by the owner and an example of how our farms were stocked before fields started to grow black and white leather wall to wall.

Along the main road, there are a couple of points at which the remains of the Neath Canal can be examined, but it is not yet possible to put together a good walk along them. Effectively, the next point to aim for is Resolven at SN 826031.

Here, the Neath Canal Society are active with a trip boat, offering a chance to cruise some of the restored section. They operate at weekends from Easter to October and daily during the main school holidays.

There is a launching slip for boats that have been trailed from elsewhere and a restored lock. The whole area won a Civic Trust award – Britain's top environmental award – in 1992.

From here to Ysgwrfa, boats can be seen. The towing path is excellent as the canal heads towards the first lock at Crugai, less than a mile away, followed in quick succession by Rheola Lock. A huge edifice to the left is owned by Consolidated Coal plc who produce and supply quality Welsh coal: a rare commodity these days. This was once an aluminium works.

A standard stone bridge is followed by something of an oddity. This had stone built abutments but the platform is of cast iron. The towing path passes underneath in the approved fashion, but it is also possible to walk up and over the top. A low level aqueduct takes the canal over a small river en route to Aberyclwyd Lock. A wooded glade is ahead, with the road on the left about to move away. Sadly, the new road is now alongside right, the peace of this section lost forever.

Beyond the trees, the valley opens out in all its glory. The steep sided hills are thick with trees and even higher hills lie ahead: dramatic. The next lock – Ynys-yr-Allor – is about half a mile away.

The restored Neath Canal at Resolven.

At Maesgwyn Lock, a stark stone ruin was once a lime kiln where limestone was burnt so that it could be spread on fields hereabouts. Approaching the end of the navigable section, some 300 yards ahead is Ysgwrfa lock. Leave the canal here, cross the busy main road and a scramble up the bank at the far side will reveal a very derelict lock.

The canal's channel continues alongside the road, past another lock and off towards Glyn Neath. The channel is narrow, reflecting encroachment from the road, but still in water. Past another lock, the main road bears right to bypass Glyn Neath, whilst this exploration follows the left hand path. But not for very far. Just before The Lamb and Flag pub, the channel disappears, making a somewhat unceremonious end to the Neath Canal.

From here, it moved in the direction of the Glyn Neath bypass which buried the route and at least three locks before the final basin area. Gone, but, possibly, not for ever.

Now the new road is in place, this old bypass is redundant and there are plans to tear it up. This will leave derelict land, under which who knows what treasures may be discovered, The local council are making favourable noises and it is not beyond the realms of possibility that this remaining section will also be re-constructed. No time scale is envisaged at the moment, and it is certainly not an imminent project; just one to watch in the future.

Local Support Group

In the van of this ambitious restoration is the Neath and Tennent Canals Preservation Society. When proposals for the new road up the valley were first announced, the route would have used much of the canal, effectively destroying it. Intensive lobbying and sheer hard work from this small society saw the scheme changed and the canal saved. Complete restoration is now entirely practical, awaiting only time and money. The NTCPS operates the trip boat at Resolven and can be contacted at 16, Gower Road, Sketty, Swansea SA2 9BY – 01792 201594.

Public Transport

Between Neath and Briton Ferry, routes X5, 156 and 227 operate. North, the X5 runs up the valley past Clyne to Resolven and then moves to the left hand side to reach Glyn Neath. This provides a lovely set of options for return transport. Full service details on 01792 580580.

Maps

Ordnance Survey Landranger series maps 170 and 160 cover the route of the canal. The *Swansea A to Z* (Geographers Ltd., – 01732 781000) also includes the canal from its southern end to just beyond Aberdulais aqueduct. This scale is 1:15840 (4 inches to 1 mile).

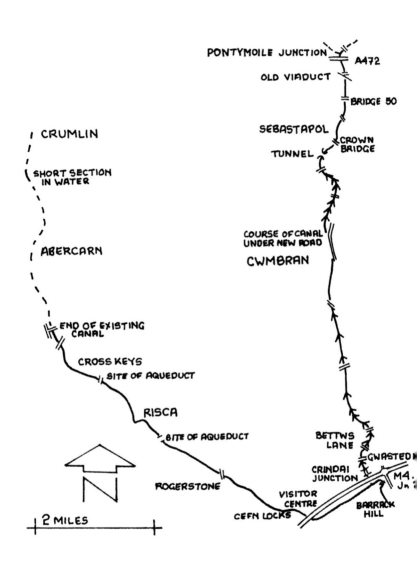

PONTYMOILE JUNCTION   A472

OLD VIADUCT

BRIDGE 50

SEBASTAPOL

TUNNEL   CROWN BRIDGE

CRUMLIN

SHORT SECTION IN WATER

COURSE OF CANAL UNDER NEW ROAD

CWMBRAN

ABERCARN

END OF EXISTING CANAL

CROSS KEYS

SITE OF AQUEDUCT

RISCA

SITE OF AQUEDUCT

BETTWS LANE

GWASTED

CRINDAI JUNCTION

M4 Jn

ROGERSTONE

VISITOR CENTRE

CEFN LOCKS

BARRACK HILL

N

2 MILES

5. The Monmouthshire Canal

Then ...

By 1791, producers at the eastern end of the ironstone and coal belt were agitating for transport. Both the Ebbw and Usk Valleys were suggested as possible routes for a canal. Newport was established as a port and a seemingly sensible destination for the projected waterway.

In the event, both valleys were served. With local landowners and a banker as main shareholders, The Monmouthshire Canal was promoted and received its parliamentary Act in 1792. It was planned to construct a navigable cut from the river Usk at Newport to Pontnewynydd, north-west of Pontypool, with a branch to Crumlin in the Ebbw Valley. Main line and branch would each be 11 miles (17.7km) long.

Because many of the potential sites for traffic were inaccessible by water, the company's Act allowed them to build a series of linking tramroads. Thus were Beaufort, Blaenavon, Sirhowy and Trosnant to be brought into the canal age.

Construction was long and difficult. The younger Dadford was appointed Engineer but, possibly having learnt from mistakes by other canals, he was expressly forbidden by the company from being involved in the contracting side.

From Newport to Crindau, almost where the M4 now runs, there was but one lock. From there, the main line rose 435ft (132.6m) along the way with flights of locks at Tŷ-coch (10), Cwmbrân (10), Pontnewydd (5) and Pontymoile (11). Other major works were three tunnels, two of which were in Newport and one at Cwmbrân.

A 358ft (109m) rise on the Crumlin Branch needed flights at Allt-yr-ynn (5), Cefn (14) and 7 at Abercarn. These were built to accommodate boats measuring 64ft 9ins with a 9ft 2in beam (19.6m x 2.8m) which would carry around 27 tonnes.

A short length at the far end of the Crumlin branch was in water by 1794, but the main line was creating problems; solid rock was costing far more to cut than had been anticipated. The project went way over budget. Money was tight and shareholders were asked to contribute further funds.

That old dictum, "The more things change, the more they remain the same", applies to civil engineering if nothing else. Two centuries later, with computers and all the panoply of modern technology, projects like the Channel Tunnel still grossly exceed both schedule and budget, causing great grief to those involved financially.

By 1796, most of the main line was navigable: after a fashion. Toll income was starting to flow, bringing blessed relief to the parlous finances. The Crumlin branch was not yet linked to the main line, neither were many of the tramroads. These would eventually provide the lifeblood for this fledgling canal.

Activity "up the valleys" saw similar action in Newport. The original quays in town were to prove woefully inadequate for the amount of trade promised by the company. Shipping tied up as close to Newport town bridge as it could get.

Pontymoile where the Brecknock & Abergavenny Canal met the Monmoutshire.

An Act of 1835 established Commissioners for the port and a new dock was built, known as Town Dock. This worked alongside the river quays, but was never as popular with canal boats.

The Monmouthshire Canal's profitability was assured by some astute management over the years. The first shrewd move was made within a few months of gaining their Act. A company further north, The Brecknock and Abergavenny (see Chapter Six) applied for – and obtained – an Act in 1793 to link Brecon with the Usk at Caerllion, just above Newport.

By dint of skilful negotiation, the latter company was persuaded to re-route their canal to make an end-on junction with the Monmouthshire near Pontypool. This ensured that all traffic originating to the north would pay tolls for use of the Monmouthshire on their way to the coast.

Although the arrangement suited both companies at the time, it was not without its difficulties later. Several acrimonious disputes occurred over the years. Some were caused by ironmasters whose location was such that they had access to either canal. Seeing the advantage of playing one against the other, these people acted hard to get, causing both canal companies to use price cutting as a means of grabbing traffic. The main tonnage was coal. In the early years of the 19th century, over 100,000 tonnes a years was reaching Newport for forwarding by ship.

But the real ace in the Monmouthshire's hand was its tramways. At the height of activity in the 1830s, the company owned well over 40 miles (65km) of them. Add to that an even greater length of privately built ones and their contribution to the well-being of the canal company can be gauged.

Not that this income was achieved without a fight. The owners of these private tramroads disliked having to pay canal company dues and the latter's legal team seemed to be constantly at work defending their interests in court.

One tramway – this one owned by the canal – actually duplicated the Crumlin canal line. There was so much traffic to be handled that the canal alone was incapable. Another company tramroad was the one from Pontymoile to Blaenavon. This was a development created by lack of

Lengthmans cottage at Pontymoile Junction.

water in the canal above Pontymoile as well as the desire to tap hitherto
virgin areas further up the valley.

In 1810, a tramroad from Trosnant to Pontypool had been extended
along the canal to allow access to boats below the flight of locks. By 1829,
the Blaenavon one that reached the canal at Pontnewydd was lengthened
to connect with the Trosnant, following the line of the canal. For a while,
trade continued along both, but the unequal struggle was halted in 1849
when the canal above Pontypool was closed. The remaining short length
down to the junction at Pontymoile closed four years later.

The Monmouthshire Canal Company, ever defensive of its turf, took
a keen interest in the development of railways, as did competing
companies. Here was a very lucrative market; by 1846, almost 1m tonnes
of cargo a year was moving along the canal and its tramways.

There were numerous proposals and counter-proposals from both the
canal company and newly established competing railway promoters. Acts
were granted, but nothing was actually built.

An amending Act of 1848 saw the company change its name to The Monmouthshire Railway and Canal Company. Several further Acts saw the financial structure changed, and various railway building took place over the next decade. That this was so much more convenient for users is clear from the fact that, by 1865, waterborne traffic yielded only a miserly £1,200 in toll revenue.

In September 1865, the Brecknock and Abergavenny was taken over by the Monmouthshire. The purpose of this move was to obtain access to the remaining traffic on that canal. Not that it moved by water. The company was, by now, fully committed to railways. The combined toll from both waterways was not enough to pay for canal maintenance.

The company tried to close the lower end around Newport in 1871, but failed. They tried again in 1879, stating that the bottom mile or so had been unused for five years. This was then granted.

But, just as the bigger canal company gobbled up the smaller one, so was "big brother" in the shape of The Great Western Railway encroaching into south Wales generally. Finally, their increasing presence in the area produced an amalgamation between the two on August 1st 1880.

The GWR had little time for this, or any other canal they were involved with. They wanted such trade as could be garnered, but not the responsibility for maintenance. Indeed, the whole business of railways acquiring canal companies and then abandoning them had created such a scandal that, in 1873, the Regulation of Railways Act had included in section 17 an obligation on railway companies to keep their canals:

"...in good working condition, navigable for the use of all persons desirous to use and navigate them without any undue hindrance, interruption or delay".

Any remaining trade diminished rapidly by the start of the 20th century. The last recorded traffic on the Crumlin Branch was in 1930, on the main line, 1938.

From then on, a series of parliamentary Acts saw successive lengths legally abandoned. Some of the canal around Cwmbrân was closed to through traffic in 1954. Bridges in the town were demolished, and culverts provided for the water to flow. Locks in the town were converted to weirs. With navigation now impossible below Cwmbrân, full closure of the original Monmouthshire length to Pontypool was effected in 1962.

And Now …

That the line of this canal is more or less extant is down to the fact that the channel was used for water supply. There were several factories along the route drawing their supplies, and Newport Docks also depended on this water, drawn from the river Usk at Brecon. The towing path is in excellent condition almost throughout and is quite suitable for disabled in wheelchairs.

Exploring from the south, the canal in Newport town centre has disappeared under a variety of road schemes and new building. The nearest point to the original end is almost a mile to the north at Barrack Hill. Leaving Newport town centre on the A4051, turn left at the huge traffic island with the Old Rising Sun pub on the right and the Lex Rover garage on the left. A sign pointing to "Raglan Barracks T.A. Centre" shows the way. Around a sharp right hand bend the road starts to climb and the towing path is on the right at ST 308892.

Although this is still very urban, there is little to suggest this from the path. The steep bosky slopes of Barracks Hill are on the left and a screen of trees protects the walker from housing. And instantly, the "Canal Effect" is there. Peace and tranquillity reign, although reverberations from urban life carry along on the breeze.

Crindau Bridge (No.1) is soon reached. This is a typical canal accommodation bridge, carrying a large plaque proclaiming its provenance. Shortly after, the canal takes a huge sweep towards the west as the M4 motorway arrives noisily alongside.

A short distance along is another – newer – bridge. This takes the towing path over the main line and away on the Crumlin Branch. For now, turn right here, at Crindau Junction (ST 304894), under an eerie concrete cavern formed by the motorway and cross an aqueduct.

Already, Newport is behind; green spaces are visible from each bank. Before long, Gwastad Bridge (No. 26) and lock hove into view. This is a roving bridge, taking the towing path to the left hand bank where it will stay for some time. Remarkably, the lock looks almost ready to function. Newish gates and paddle gear all intact: quite a surprise.

A quiet section of water follows, with the canal on something of an embankment passing lakes to the left. The path is tree-lined as it reaches Bettws Lane Bridge No (27) – ST 301902.

• Turn right up the hill to the main road for the Cwmbrân to Newport bus service.

Another lock lies just beyond the bridge, this time ungated and with no paddle gear. The canal is really starting to weave now as it struggles to hold the contour against an ever climbing valley. Ahead, hills start to be noticed as the towing path continues out into the countryside.

Intriguing mix of architecture on the Monmouthshire Canal. An accommodation bridge crosses the canal whilst a disused railway viaduct runs alongside.

At the next road crossing, a small unclassified one, the bridge been flattened and canal infilled by the road. Another lock chamber is soon encountered, followed shortly by another. Both have sound masonry but are ungated.

Picnic tables and a very tidy area hail the next locks, two very close together followed by another a short distance further along. At the tail of the next lock stands a very attractive stone bridge, barely wide enough for pedestrians, but very substantially built. A huge concrete road bridge follows. The main arch takes the water, pedestrians take the smaller arch to the left. There is another lock here as the canal continues to climb towards Cwmbrân.

Another chamber precedes another culverted bridge and then Cwmbrân is starting to make its presence felt with an industrial area to the right. Another lock precedes a short infilled section. Where the towing path meets the road, walk straight across along a small road. This carries no name but has a "Parks and Nursery Depot" on the left hand corner.

One hundred yards along and water is discovered again – albeit not for long. Follow the towing path – still on the left – until the canal comes to an end (ST 292948). The path is a cycleway here; follow it to the road and turn right along Commercial Street.

A bridge takes this road over a busy new road below. The construction of this took away the line of the canal completely, although it can be picked up some 500 yards along. After the bridge, at the next junction, turn left down a hill. On the right is Cwmbrân Village Surgery and opposite, on the left, a path down to the new road, Cwmbrân Drive.

• Carry straight on here into Cwmbrân and the bus depot.

Follow the main road to a traffic island, then cross to the left hand footpath. Carry straight on at the island and just beyond, on the left by a B & Q supermarket, up a slight bank, the water is re-discovered.

A towing path re-appears, this time on the right hand side which soon diverges from the frenetic traffic along the road. This section lasts for only a few yards before another infilled section is encountered. The route is clear to follow, to the left hand side of two modern factories.

This is the flight of Cwmbrân Locks, raising the canal steeply up the side of a hill. A pub, The New Bridgend, stands alongside the towing path and is a nice place for refreshment. Housing still crowds both sides of the canal, adding nothing to the milieu.

Pontnewydd brings further locks and further infilling. The area here has been made thoroughly attractive by tree planting, grassing and cascading of the lock chambers.

Beyond these, more tree-lined towing path with the canal on an

Crindau bridge, Monmouthshire Canal.

embankment. After a gentle "S" bend, a flight of five locks is reached with a small aqueduct just before the bottom chamber.

Above the top lock, civilisation is instantly left behind as rolling hills dominate the view. The Brecon Beacons National Park is now but a short distance away. This section of canal was re-opened to navigation in 1995 after the rebuilding of a bridge further along. A short (87 yard) tunnel is located in the same glorious open countryside.

Sebastopol, and Crown Bridge (No 48) at ST 293983 was culverted when the canal was closed. It has now been rebuilt in an attractive form and was the blockage referred to earlier. The eponymous pub is across the water, with a fish and chip shop close by.

• Turn right towards the bus stop back to Cwmbrân.

A few yards further along on the towing path side, The Open Hearth serves Ansells Ales. Take note, on reaching bridge 50, that there is restricted headroom and tall walkers need to be very careful. An old railway viaduct crosses high overhead and a small accommodation bridge over the canal makes for a very attractive location.

A huge concrete road bridge leads to Pontymoile Junction (SO 293003), with its traditional stone bridge making a fine contrast. The old Pontymoile line led off to the left here, up the Lwyd valley, but there is effectively nothing of this 1 mile/11 lock line to be found. From here, the canal is the Brecknock and Abergavenny line which is explored in detail during Chapter Six.

• Leave the canal over the stone bridge and walk past the stone building into a narrow road. Follow this for some 250 yards to a large traffic island and one-way system. Walk against the flow of traffic to the bus stop for Cwmbrân.

Returning to Crindau Junction, the Crumlin Branch continues alongside the motorway for a short distance before sweeping away towards a series of four locks that lift the canal gently. Although not close by, the M4 still makes its presence felt by the noise level. But not for long. The canal turns sharp right, dives under the road and starts to climb.

Cefn Locks are probably the most impressive piece of canal engineering in south Wales, lifting the canal 168 feet (51m) through fourteen locks arranged in seven pairs. These are not true staircase locks, where the chambers are physically linked. Here, each has a few feet of water between gates. This technique was seldom used in canal construction, but was employed at Bratch, on the Staffs and Worcester canal where Dadford Snr. learnt his trade. The main benefit to be gained is water economy. Each top lock drains into a side pond, thus saving it all for the next occasion that the chamber below is filled.

There is an attractive, white painted former lock keeper's cottage halfway up the flight, at which point the towing path moves to the left hand bank where it will remain.

At the top of this flight (ST 279886), a visitor centre has been established together with car park. The whole area is well populated by people looking at this remarkable flight. And, having climbed the hill, the canal retains this level for the rest of the available distance.

• Turn left and walk down to the main road for a bus to Newport.

Leaving the flight behind, the canal enters a short cutting before bearing to the left to make the acquaintance of Cefn Road in Rogerstone. A pub, The Rising Sun, sells Courage ales. This will be the last "watering hole" encountered on this canal so, if a thirst beckons, quench it.

Wildlife along this canal is rich and varied. Swan, mallard, and moorhen are discovered frequently. Kingfisher and heron less so, but their presence adds to the deep pleasure of exploring this length.

Derelict locks on the Cefn flight, Monmouthshire Canal, Crumlin Branch.

An aqueduct taking the water over Manor Road, Tŷ-Sign, has been removed and the water ends for a short while as the path drops down to the road and up the other side. On the right is a newsagents and fish and chip shop. Another flattened bridge sees the road crossing at water level as the remaining canal water is piped through.

One stone bridge on this length has the most dramatic stalactites forming on the underside of the arch. Then the canal peters out. Ahead, Darren Road. This is a re-alignment of the original road and caused the destruction of a fine aqueduct. Continue in a similar direction and regain the towing path – and water – at the top of a short bank.

• Drop down the steep hill to the road at the bottom for a bus to Newport.

The course continues high on the eastern side of the Ebbw valley as the canal clings precariously to the contour. Below, rooftops of both

Lockside furniture like this bollard have been preserved wherever possible on the Monmouthshire Canal.

houses and factories and a gentle wash of noise. Up on the towing path, peace and seclusion. At several points along here, stabilisation work has taken place to ensure that the whole edifice does not go washing down on to the road and railway below. A length on the Llangollen Canal did just that in similar circumstances – see Chapter Twelve.

The end of the canal is reached quite suddenly at the southern edge of Cwmcarn (ST 219931). From here, the route of the canal has been destroyed, largely by road improvements. There is a short section just outside Newbridge at ST 215962, a tree-lined length to the left of the main road, but that is, effectively, all there is to be seen.

Maps

Ordnance Survey map 171 covers the whole of this canal. The lower reaches are featured in the *Geographer's A to Z of Cardiff* mentioned in Chapter Three.

Public Transport

There is ample public transport covering both routes. The service providers are:

Stagecoach Red and White
Tel: (01633) 266336

Glyn Williams Travel
Tel: (01495) 229237

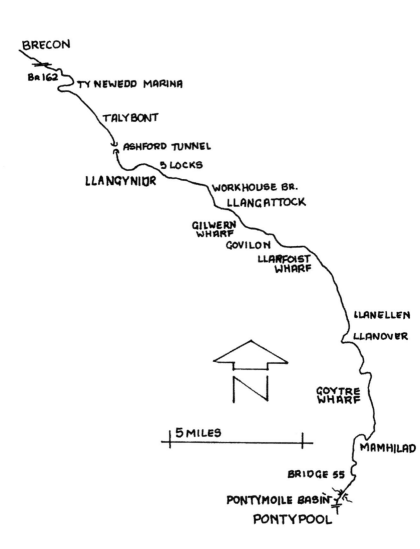

BRECON

BR 162

TY NEWEDD MARINA

TALYBONT

ASHFORD TUNNEL

5 LOCKS

LLANGYNIUR

WORKHOUSE BR.

LLANGATTOCK

GILWERN WHARF

GOVILON

LLANFOIST WHARF

LLANELLEN

LLANOVER

GOYTRE WHARF

5 MILES

MAMHILAD

BRIDGE 55

PONTYMOILE BASIN

PONTYPOOL

6. The Brecknock and Abergavenny Canal

Then ...

The promoters of this canal – originally known as The Abergavenny Canal – employed the younger Dadford to survey a line in 1792. The original thinking had been to build a canal from the river Usk at Newbridge, five miles (8km) north-west of Caerleon, following roughly the line of the river to Glangrwyne near Gilwern. There were ironworks in this area and prospects for trade seemed quite reasonable. Further deliberations produced an expanded plan that would see the line extended further up the valley to Brecon.

The committee of the Monmouthshire heard of this proposal and quickly arranged a meeting with the B & M promoters. The outcome of this was that the proposed line would be altered quite dramatically. It would make an end-on junction with the Monmouthshire at Pontymoile and run to Brecon.

An Act was obtained in 1793 and the company formally established. Also included – in common with the Monmouthshire – was provision for tramways to be built up to eight miles (12.9km) from the line of the canal. Unusually for Welsh waterways, it was very much a "canal of the people". Big investors were not too prominent. Several of the major players in the Monmouthshire enterprise also staked in this canal, but essentially, the main funds came from locals.

Following the granting of the Act, there appears to have been something of an hiatus. The first signs of construction appeared in 1794 (or 1796, depending on whose interpretation of history is the most accurate), when a tramway was opened. This was to carry coal from Gellifelen colliery near Brynmawr to Glangrwyne on the east side of the Usk, the originally planned destination of the canal.

The Brecknock and Abergavenny Canal at Llanfoist.

Further tramroads were constructed to the west beyond Gellifelen, but of water there was no sign. It was to be the early weeks of 1797 before actual canal construction began. Thomas Dadford was engaged as engineer on a part-time basis – he was still busy on the Monmouthshire – and Gilwern heading north-west was the first section to be built.

This work included five locks at Llangynidr, a 375 yard (343m) tunnel near Talybont, a superb four-arched stone aqueduct over the Usk at Brynich and a further lock beyond. The chambers were built for boats 64ft 9ins by 9ft 2ins (19.2m x 2.8m).

Considering the dramatically steep countryside hereabouts, it really is quite remarkable that the canal could run over 33 miles (53.3km) between Pontypool and Brecon, climbing just 60ft (18.3m) in so doing. It was achieved by the simple process of hugging the west side of the Usk valley. When it bends, so does the canal. In doing so it twists and turns like a snake on speed, giving the impression that it has lost its way to Brecon.

By Christmas 1798, the canal was built almost to Talybont. Funds were short, and shareholders were asked to stump up more cash. This enabled the work to reach Brecon. On a crisp Wednesday morning, Christmas Eve 1800, the canal was opened.

But of the southward extension towards the Monmouthshire there was nothing. The tramways by now were creating a cash flow, and the opportunity to progress was grasped. This was a most opportune moment. The Monmouthshire were making litigious noises about the failure of the new canal to connect with theirs. They had paid good money up front for this and were getting quite cross at their perceived loss of income.

Thomas Dadford had moved on and an engineer from the Worcester and Birmingham Canal, Thomas Cartwright, was engaged to re-survey the line. This burst of activity soon foundered on the financial rocks as Llanfoist was reached. It needed a substantial loan from several vested interests – particularly Richard Crawshay whom we met in Chapter Three – before yet another engineer – William Crosley Jnr. – was engaged to complete the work. He started from the Pontymoile end (perhaps to give the Monmouthshire proprietors something to see), building a stop lock and rebuilding an aqueduct.

Eventually, on Friday February 7th 1812, to great rejoicing, the canal was declared open. And anything to rejoice at must have been more than welcome in those dark days. It was the year when Napoleon, having invaded Russia, began his ignominious retreat. The Luddites were still creating havoc around England, and Prime Minster Spencer Perceval was assassinated in the House of Commons.

But any jubilation was not long-lived. The delays had seen the B & A miss the financial jackpot. Peace broke out following the defeat of Napoleon and the munitions industry, which needed masses of iron, resumed its peacetime role; one of much less intense consumption of raw materials.

There were still tramroads under construction, both under the auspices of the B & A and by private owners. The Bryn-oer was one such. Leaving the canal at Talybont, it ran almost south up the Caerfanell valley before turning left to climb over Mynydd Llangynidr servicing quarries at Trevil before reaching Man-y-bwch, Princetown and Bryn-oer.

Llanfoist Wharf, Brecknock and Abergavenny Canal.

The Rhymney Ironworks was also served. Another, to Hereford, was eventually replaced by a "proper" railway, as was another one to Hay-on-Wye.

Lack of return to the shareholders prompted questions from these long-suffering individuals. Faced with a relatively lightly used system, the directors tried several initiatives in an attempt to stimulate traffic. Raw materials free one way on the understanding that finished goods would return along the canal was tried, albeit with limited success. Staff wages were cut in 1821, and again in 1822. This saw a marginal increase in profits, which were further improved over the next few years as some trade expanded and wages were increased.

In truth, there really was too much carrying capacity for the amount of available trade. This was highlighted when the Monmouthshire opened extensions to their tramway system, creaming off much of the B & A's trade in the Nantyglo area. Then in 1836, the former's Rumney Tramroad was opened and much of the stone trade from the Bryn-oer decamped.

Times were getting desperate. Realising that they could not fight the Monmouthshire, exploratory talks were instituted by the B & A to try to create some form of working agreement. Bargaining with their backs to the wall, they had to accept the best deal they could. After several abortive attempts to deal with other fledgling railway companies, this, as mentioned in Chapter Five, was an amalgamation with the MCC.

From this point, its history is inextricably linked to the Monmouthshire. After the Great Western Railway took over the amalgamated lines it became known as the Monmouthshire and Brecon Canal.

The last commercial trade was recorded in 1933, but the whole line was retained as a water channel. After the 1939-45 war, the interest in pleasure boating grew, and nowhere more so than on this gloriously attractive canal.

Indeed, it was its very location that proved the salvation. After the creation of the Brecon Beacons National Park, the potential for this canal was realised. Covering 519 square miles (1344km²), virtually all the canal lies within this park, and it didn't take long before restoration ideas were being considered.

Local councils became involved along with British Waterways: the then unenlightened BW who had not yet come to terms with canal conservation. It must have taken an almighty effort to shift this behemoth into action. But shift it did.

In 1964 work started on the Llangynidr lock chambers. The long process was completed in 1970 when a new lift bridge at Talybont was installed, replacing the fixed structure just a few inches above water level that had been installed after the original closure. That meant that the whole of the old Brecknock and Abergavenny line was available to boat and walker, together with the upper reaches of the Monmouthshire.

For many years, effective navigation ended at Pontymoile. Then in 1995, a bridge in Sebastopol was rebuilt and the canal dredged. This now allows boats almost to Cwmbrân, although walkers have always been able to get that far. Two miles of the Monmouthshire Canal are now restored, and work continues to open more.

And Now ...

With all the canal open to boats and the towing path in good condition throughout, the thirty three mile (53km) exploration is quite easy, but transport is irregular; see note at the end of this chapter.

There are many canals which boast glorious views, but for sustained grandeur, this canal leaves them all standing. Several of the mountains hereabouts clear 1500ft (457m). The broad valley of the river Usk is to the right, whilst the bulk of Craig y Fan to the left reaches in excess of 2,000ft (609m).

For the first dozen miles (19.2km) the canal forms a boundary for The Brecon Beacons National Park: neither in nor out. Each little stream flowing to join the mighty Usk is crossed by an aqueduct, and many villages along the way are almost ignored.

But this has its advantages for the explorer. These frequent turns bring an ever changing vista over this magnificent valley. There are little stone bridges, seemingly every few yards; all adding to the charm of this waterway.

There is a pub in Pontymoile, just a short distance right of bridge 55, but this is the only refreshment for several miles. A boatyard at Goetre offers hire craft for the day or week, and there are the remains of old lime kilns there as well.

Again, the canal avoids the actual village, as it does through Llanover, Llanellen and Llanfoist. This is a delightfully charming section, still high above the river, but with enchantingly restored buildings on the old wharf.

• Leave the canal here. Note the engraving on step number four: B & A Co. Walk down the track to the bottom. At the main road turn right, and about 200 yards along opposite the Llanfoist Inn, the X4 service back to Abergavenny and then Pontypool stops.

The mass of Blorenge Carn is on the left, and the canal picks its way around the base of it. As the canal takes a very sharp right, it finally enters the National Park.

Still wooded and, for a short time at least, not offering the quality of views, the canal continues its peaceful way towards Brecon. That peace is broken around Govilon where British Waterways have their yard and a visitor centre along with a line of moored boats.

One of these is the trip boat WILLIAM DE BRAOSE. The towing path moves to the left hand side for a short distance. Here, the village is somewhat closer to the canal. At the end of this section, the towing path returns to the right bank and The Bridge End is a pub close by the aqueduct. On this bridge is an unusual shop: a butchers with general groceries and ice cream.

Brecknock and Abergavenny Canal.

More refreshment just over a mile (2km) away at Gilwern. But before that, the busy Heads of the Valleys road runs alongside the canal, destroying the peace that reigned for so long. But that soon heads away west and tranquility returns. The canal passes the village and another boatyard at Gilwern Wharf. Included in their fleet are electrically powered boats.

Travelling in one of these is a delight. The motor imparts an almost inaudible whine, the water bubbles a little at the back where it is churned by the propeller: otherwise, silence. It's even quieter than a horse-drawn boat. There, the beat of hoofs on the ground, pleasant though it may sound, still warns wildlife. In one of these, it is possible to creep up unannounced on a variety of animals and birds.

There are the remains of a wharf at Workhouse Bridge (118), and another at Ffawyddog. Here, stone from a nearby quarry would be loaded into boats for delivery, usually to the south.

This is Black Mountain country. The valley is quite narrow here, with steep hills quite close at each side. Myarth on the right falls away quickly into Glanusk Park, whilst on the left, Cwm Claisfer

The Brecknock and Abergavenny Canal at Llanfoist.

gives way to the bulk of Mynydd Llangynidr, 2000ft high (609m).

Now, there is a road that has discovered the canal and decided to keep it company for much of the way to Brecon. The canal swings left to skirt Llangattock Park and keeps well to the west of that village. Again, more industrial archaeology is on display at the wharf.

The valley broadens out here and the canal enters a long tree-lined section. Beauty really is all around. Another aqueduct precedes a right turn which takes the canal away from Llangattock and towards Cwm Crawnon where the first locks are encountered.

This area was once riddled with caves and quarries. Limestone was a vital ingredient in the iron smelting process carried on along the south

Wales coast and provided plenty of trade for the canal. The scenery now turns a little more friendly, with some land being farmed. A cone-shaped hill to the right is the National Trust owned Sugar Loaf, 2,000ft (609m) high, with rhododendron bushes creating a mass of colour during the season.

• Leave the canal just beyond the first lock and turn left at the main road towards the Coach & Horses. The bus stops here. Note also, there is liquid refreshment as well as a bus.

Four more locks lift the canal to its penultimate level. The canal's only tunnel at Ashford is 375 yards (343m) long without a towing path; take the road over the top.

Talybont approaches. The Star Inn is canalside and there are shops easily accessed by the electric lift bridge. This section was the site of a serious breach in December 1994. The towpath just gave way, releasing the contents of the canal into the houses lower down. A sterling effort by British Waterways staff contained the damage and a concrete liner installed to preclude any repetition. Subsequently, BW engineers have been investigating the stability of this whole length in an effort to avoid a repeat.

• The Abergavenny bus stops here.

A series of pretty lift bridges punctuate this section and the canal manages to keep something of a straight course, quite remarkable considering the terrain and what has gone before.

A newly reconstructed aqueduct takes the canal across the river Menascin. Then, a few houses mark the hamlet of Pencelli before the canal heads off left to turn sharp right under the road.

This is the base of a horse drawn trip boat. DRAGONS TAIL is a sturdy old iron canal boat, and Merlin the friendly horse. Operator Alan Picken lives in the converted Old Store House. He is a gifted artist, painting some delightful canal scenes. Also in the building is a small museum containing a diverse collection of canal history, including some of the original Acts of Parliament authorising the construction of canals.

This is also the home of a nationally known piece of canal decoration. The old boatman's style of painted roses and castles adorning narrowboats

The Brecknock and Abergavenny Canal at Llanover.

all over the country are expensive and time consuming to produce. Also operating a small screen printing business, Alan came up with the answer. He created one set of decorations and turned them into water-based transfers. He has been churning them out for over twenty years now, and they can be seen on hundreds of canal boats all over the country. Their popularity seems boundless.

Beyond bridge 159 is the (fairly) new marina and hire boat base at Tŷ Newydd. The line curves back to the left giving the most dramatic views over real hills. It's almost becoming schizoid now, this section: delicate and intimate around the waterside, big, bold and brash on the horizon. Whatever it is, it's truly stunning.

And the adjectives are not over yet. Tumbling away far below the towpath is the river Usk. The bank between the towpath and river is quite sheer, meaning that you can look down into the river and spot salmon leaping up the weir. There aren't too many canals to offer this treat. Or a really striking aqueduct. There are many on this line, but none finer than the one that now takes the canal over the Usk. Just before this, the towpath changes sides at bridge 162. Be careful here, as the path appears to carry on along the right hand bank.

After this quite breathtaking crossing, a sharp left brings the path to Brynich Lock. Beautifully maintained, with carefully tended flower beds and hanging baskets, there are even bits of traditional canal decoration applied to the paddle gear; it really is the perfect accompaniment to what has gone before.

From here, the outskirts of Brecon become apparent. The town's by-pass crosses overhead and fields slope gently down to the river on the left. All too soon, the canal finishes. A sanitary station, small winding hole, a box to allow the recharging of electric boats and it is all over.

This is the new basin area, created in time for the 1997 season. This is also the location of Theatr Brycheiniog. Offering theatre together with a whole range of entertainments, Theatr Brycheiniog is set to become the entertainments focus for this corner of Powys. The annual Jazz festival in town will be putting the new facilities to good use.

Opened in April 1997, there is a café and bar, a gallery and rehearsal room within the complex. The £7m project was jointly funded by EC Regional Development and the Arts Council Lottery Scheme on land owned by British Waterways and Powys County Council.

Walk beyond the head of navigation for a few yards and take the first right by Brecon Motors. Turn left at the end, and bear right after 300 yards (274m) for the Square and the Wellington Hotel. The bus departs from here.

As a postscript: if you feel that the superlatives used to describe this exploration are a little overdone, please reserve judgement until after your visit. You will then be busy searching the thesaurus for new ones.

Public Transport

Bus services for one-way walks are variable in quality and there is no train service, so this must have some bearing on your plans. From Pontymoile to Llanfoist (for Abergavenny) is a twelve mile (19.2km) hike. From Llangattock to Brecon, a very infrequent service runs roughly along the canal's route back to Abergavenny making the whole thing a little hit-or-miss. But, with careful planning, the whole of this dramatic canal can be yours. Red and White Bus service 20 runs from Brecon to Abergavenny. Details of this and the Abergavenny to Pontypool service on 01633 485118.

Maps

Ordnance Survey Landranger sheets 160, 161 and 171.

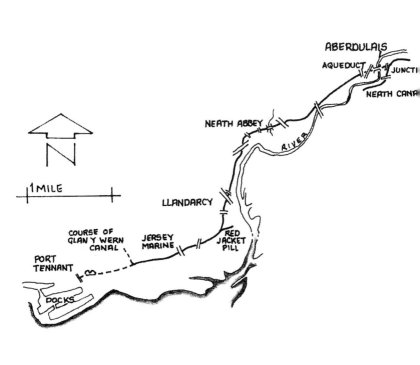

ABERDULAIS

AQUEDUCT

JUNCTI

NEATH CANA

NEATH ABBEY

RIVER

1 MILE

LLANDARCY

COURSE OF
GLAN Y WERN
CANAL

JERSEY
MARINE

RED
JACKET
PILL

PORT
TENNANT

DOCKS

7. The Tennant Canal

Then ...

The tale of two previously examined canals, the Brecknock and Abergavenny and the Monmouthshire (Chapters Five and Six) gives the impression that they were inextricably linked – although they were independent for many years. The Tennant offers a relationship with the Neath (Chapter Four) of almost incestuous character, but one that would see both companies steadfastly independent throughout their existence.

Although the actual Tennant Canal (a.k.a. The Neath and Swansea Junction Canal) dates from 1824, there was considerable waterway activity prior to that date. In 1790, the owner of Glan-y-Wern colliery, halfway between Swansea and Neath, built a canal to link his pit with the river Neath at Red Jacket Pill. This 3½ mile (5.6km) long, lock-free line had to cross the Crymlyn Bog, a huge natural hazard in those days. The Pill currently lies under the M4 link roads to junction 42 near Llandarcy.

The canal did not make a physical connection with the river, and after the colliery owner – Edward Elton – was declared bankrupt, the canal fell into disuse.

George Tennant was a Lancashire lad who came to live in south Wales. He bought an estate at Rydding, on the north east edge of Neath, in 1816. He took an interest in the canal, obtained a lease from the then owner, Lord Vernon, and proceeded to clean it out and make a lock into the river. He also planned to build a further canal westwards from the Glan-y-wern towards the river Tawe at Swansea. Tennant could already see that the Tawe estuary offered far more potential to shippers than did the Neath.

This was to become known as The Red Jacket Canal, again a.k.a. The Neath and Swansea Junction. In total, it was 4 miles (6.4km) long, again, with no locks, other than into the river, and the project was overseen by William Kirkhouse, a mining engineer from Llanelli. There was some traffic on it which appreciated the access to Swansea, but not enough to repay Tennant's investment. Something more was needed, and traffic on the Neath canal caught his eye.

The ruins of Neath Abbey alongside the Tennant Canal.

Our George was quite a dynamic sort of chap: foolish, some would say. Spotting the source of his future wealth, he started looking at ways to connect. His first thought was to approach the Neath company for permission to build a lock at Giants Grave, opposite his Red Jacket lock and get the boats to cross the river into his canal. But, no sooner had he proposed that than a further development took his fancy.

In 1820, he decided to build a new canal along the west bank of the Neath to Aberdulais, there to join the Neath canal. He was so convinced that this would be his salvation that, in his enthusiasm, he started work without an Act of Parliament.

This meant that he had no powers of compulsory purchase. Perhaps he expected co-operation and investment from the landowners concerned: but he didn't get it. One gentleman who had earlier promised a short stretch of land around the Neath to Swansea road changed his mind. No amount of coercion could make him budge. The work reached his land in 1821 and there it stopped.

It took a full year of delicate conciliation involving the Neath Canal proprietors and several others who used their good offices before a deal was struck: at extremely unfavourable terms for Mr. Tennant. The total stoppage of work amounted to over eighteen months.

A bargain made, work leapt ahead. There were two major constructions required now: a lock, followed by a huge ten-arched aqueduct some 340ft (103.6m) long. From there, a short link made a junction with the Neath Canal. This was completed and opened on May 13th 1824. The extension from Red Jacket to Aberdulais was 4 miles 7 furlongs (7.8km) and accommodated boats the same size as the Neath: 60ft by 8ft 10ins (16.2m x 2.65m). What George Tennant had created was the second largest (after the Bridgewater in Lancashire) privately owned canal in the British Isles.

His interest now turned to the Swansea end. Here, on the eastern bank of the Tawe he had created Port Tennant. Sadly, the amount of work needed to improve this sufficiently to take larger ships was beyond his resources. He died in 1832 aged 67, without seeing the true results of his foresight.

Swansea decided in 1852 that a new harbour was needed. Even this long after Tennant, they still ignored his vision, building the North Dock in 1854 and the South Dock in 1859, both further up the river. It was not until wiser counsels prevailed that the Prince of Wales Dock was opened where the north arm of the canal terminated in Port Tennant. The canal had a link into this development which opened in 1881.

Since then, the Kings Dock (1909) and the Queens Dock (1920) have both been built on the site and the vision of Port Tennant, as seen by its progenitor, had finally come to be.

But there were still some improvements to be carried out on the canal. Several small arms were built, each of which provided more trade to the canal. The longest was the one mile (1.6km) Tir-isaf canal, towards the western end which linked a colliery with the main line and thence to Port Tennant. Here a copper smelting works had been established, and the fuel needed was supplied along this branch.

The Tennant Canal at Neath Abbey.

Trade continued to be good for several decades. Passenger boat workings were introduced in 1827 and survived until the coming of railways in the early 1850s. As with the Neath, much of the trade carried could not be reached by the newly built railways, and it continued to flow along the canals. This meant that the disastrous rate-cutting, applied by other canals in an effort to hang on to whatever trade they had, never applied to the Tennant. Even by 1876, they were carrying more (110,000 tonnes) than was the case forty years earlier (88,000 tonnes).

But, inevitably, this could not last. By the turn of the century, trade was disintegrating. The Tir-isaf and Glan-y-wern were closed during the Great War. A skeleton trade survived on the main line until the last war when part of the canal was damaged by enemy bombing.

Thus did the canal finally close. But, as we have seen so often, local industries had come to rely on the canal for water supplies. This proved its salvation, and the channel was maintained, with descendants of George Tennant still controlling the company which bears his name.

Which is a fitting tribute to this man. He seems to have been quite a self-deprecating character behind his business façade. He was the author of a booklet published in 1824, *Neath and Swansea, Red Jacket and Neath Canals. Narrative of Some Particulars Relating to their Formation.*

From this, and other published information, a philanthropic streak seems to be prominent. Pleased that he could provide employment for local workmen, his presence, even as an "incomer" does not seem to have been resented. But anyone with money to spend in those days must have been a welcome sight. One lady, a shopkeeper named Elizabeth Davies, even wrote a nineteen-verse poem to celebrate the opening of his canal. Just a couple of lines from this may indicate the esteem in which George Tennant was held.

"Employ to poor labourers, it is known full well,
He have them by making the Neath Junction Canal."

And Now ...

PLEASE NOTE : The Tennant Canal is privately owned and, as such, the towing path is NOT a Right of Way. However, the owners have no objection to people using the line in a proper manner. With the exception of a few yards, the whole of this canal is open for exploration.

The canal starts at Aberdulais Basin (SS 773993) at its junction with the Neath. After the few yards of basin area the water funnels into the wonderful stone aqueduct. Sadly, this is currently stanked off and water-less. There is also a fence to stop pedestrians.

Return to Dulas Fach Road and cross the metal footbridge, turning right at the end into Station Road and turn first left down Canal Side. The towing path here is in poor condition, as it will be for some distance yet.

Ahead, new bridges seem to be sprouting everywhere as road development has taken place in a mindblowing fashion. Past the new works and peace descends on the towing path. High reeds obliterate anything less pleasant to the eye.

The new road, overhead again, decides to cross the water and where it does, the towing path is very restricted in width. Approaching the edge of Neath, the line passes under a gorgeous stone bridge with setts laid into the ground. Over this, a modern metal pedestrian bridge. Here, the Neath river is close by, some fifteen feet (4.6m) vertically below. Just across the water, the Neath Canal.

At the next – steeply angled – bridge the towing path follows its own course slightly away from the water. The only problem is that the path drops down a little before climbing back again, and there is no drainage. Hence, after rain, water stands in this hollow. This is evidenced elsewhere on this canal but, in all except one case, there is a concrete edging to the canal that can be used as a footpath.

Aberdulais Aqueduct, taking the Tennant Canal over the river Neath.

A small aqueduct carries the canal over a stream in a most attractive area. Grassy fields to one side and on the right, a huge ruin, which is accessed at the next bridge.

This is Neath Abbey. It was built around 1130 and was a Cistercian order that became very wealthy. By the end of the 1300s, they farmed some 5,000 acres (2,225ha) owning many cattle and sheep. The Abbey was dissolved by Henry VIII in 1539 and the place turned into a house. That slowly fell into disrepair and in due course the site became abandoned.

Excavations between 1924 and 1935 revealed the ruins as an important window on life eight hundred years ago and they are now controlled by Cadw: Welsh Historic Monuments. Admission is free, and a useful small guide is on sale at the caretaker's cottage price 60p.

The towing path changes to the right bank at this bridge and becomes very difficult. It is used a little, but not enough. A sharp left turn takes the canal towards a main road high overhead. On reaching a flat metal bridge, cross to the left hand bank.

Soon after starting this length, a hurdle is located across the towing path. It is easily crossed, not just by walkers, but joggers, horses, motor bikes and cycles; all use this section freely and the towing path is much the better for it. From here to the end of the canal is good and firm.

At the end of an industrial complex, Red Jacket Pill is reached (SS 724947). This was the original end of the canal. Looking down the water on the left, there is ample evidence of the brickwork that used to be part of the quays here.

A hill rears up directly ahead, and the canal turns right to avoid it. On the left, more hills; a particularly attractive length of canal. Around the corner, another footbridge – quite rickety – taking the towing path to the right hand bank. Roads and industry are distant here and the low noise level is greatly to be appreciated.

The next bridge is at Jersey Marine. Yet again, the towing path changes sides; for the last time. A huge pipe bridge crosses the canal. Scrubby trees to the left hide the mass of Ford Motor works whilst the canal itself rapidly becomes blocked with reeds. On the right (SS701936), the Glan-y-Wern Canal leaves to the north but is not available for exploration.

Aberdulais Aqueduct, taking the Tennant Canal over the river Neath.

Now, there is really very little to indicate that there is a canal at all. The reeds obscure the water and the towing path leaves the water's edge for a while. Swansea lies ahead as the walk drifts away from the course of the canal as both enter a playing field. To the right is where Port Tennant was, but there is scant evidence to be seen now.

The extension into the Prince of Wales Dock does still exist for some of its original distance. Again, road reconstruction on the A483 Fabian Way has severed the actual connection, but it can be traced as the footpath joins Wern Fawr Road at SS 681932.

From here, there is little to see – at the moment. Recently, the local council conducted a feasibility study on a proposal to re-connect the Tennant with the dock area. This came out in favour of the scheme. How it will progress, only time will tell.

Local Support Group

The society encountered in Chapter Four extends its interest to this canal. The Neath and Tennant Canals Preservation Society can be contacted at 16, Gower Road, Sketty, Swansea, West Glamorgan SA2 9BY – 01792 201594.

Public Transport

The problem for walkers is that the route of this canal cuts across the usual bus routes and there is no rail service. This effectively means that the whole 8½ mile length must be walked in one go. Even then, a change of services in Neath is needed. But, with dextrous use of the map and bus timetable, shorter walks can be achieved. Details of local buses on 01792 580580

Maps

The Geographers' *A to Z Swansea Street Atlas* covers much of the lower section of this canal, including all the navigable length, at a scale of 4 inches to 1 mile (1:15840). Ordnance Survey Landranger Sheets 159, 160 and 170 cover the whole canal.

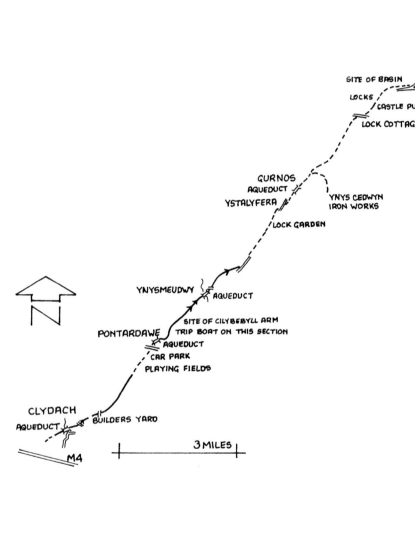

SITE OF BASIN

LOCKS

CASTLE PU

LOCK COTTAG

GURNOS
AQUEDUCT

YSTALYFERA

YNYS CEDWYN
IRON WORKS

LOCK GARDEN

YNYSMEUDWY

AQUEDUCT

SITE OF CILYBEBYLL ARM
TRIP BOAT ON THIS SECTION

PONTARDAWE

AQUEDUCT

CAR PARK

PLAYING FIELDS

CLYDACH

AQUEDUCT

BUILDERS YARD

M4

3 MILES

8. The Swansea Canal

Then ...

In common with other canals that have been examined thus far, the Swansea was created out of the need to develop transport for raw materials along a Welsh valley. It was different in that several earlier attempts to create artificial navigation at the lower end of the valley had already been undertaken. To properly appreciate the position of the Swansea in the grand scheme of things, it is first necessary to examine one of the earlier developments in this area.

Around 1790, a short canal was dug on the west shore of the Tawe from Landore up to Fforest Copper Works. It was believed to have been a joint effort by colliery owners at Landore and John Morris, co-owner of the copper plant. This gentleman later gave his name to Morriston, now a suburb of Swansea.

It was just over a mile (1.8km) long and did not have an Act of Parliament. This created some friction locally, the more so as proposals for the Swansea were launched. The canal would run for 16½ miles (26.6km) from Swansea up the Tawe valley to Heneuadd, and would include Morris's canal within its length.

But there was one vociferous objector to the Bill as laid before parliament. The Duke of Beaufort was that person, and at this distance it is impossible to put any real interpretation on his behaviour or understand the motive. Suffice it to say that, within the Act as finally passed, he was allowed to built The Trewyddfa Canal as part of the overall plan.

This, just under 1½ miles (2.2km) long, actually took over Morris's. This meant that between the rest of the upper canal and the docks was this short length of canal on which separate tolls were paid. The machinations of vested interests surrounding the birth of this canal show that there is nothing today's Boardroom could learn from those entrepreneurs save how to produce a pie chart on a computer.

There was a wharf above Morris's canal, but it could only handle ships up to 200 tonnes. The main harbour, taking vessels almost three times as large, was close to where the railway station now sits in Swansea. The Duke favoured the latter, of course. As did Morris. He feared that if coal was shipped before it reached his area, he would lose the best quality that he needed for his business.

Many of the promoters, early shareholders and committee members also had extensive interests in the Neath canal, over in the next valley – see Chapter Four. The argument raged throughout 1793 and eventually, with the Corporation strongly backing the town proposal, the Duke of Beaufort withdrew, taking his money with him. Jubilant supporters were ready to proceed until an ace appeared from up the sleeve of His Grace. Water: And the supply of same!

A 1791 Harbour Act controlled this side of things, but the duke managed to insert his very profitable oar in giving support to the Bill only after a concession on his Trewyddfa Canal.

Thereafter, an uneasy peace broke out. The Act was granted in May 1794 and Charles Roberts was appointed to build the canal. He assembled a team of direct labour and work

This was a lock. The Swansea Canal at Godre'r Graig, Ystalyfera.

began. Thomas Sheasby Snr. joined in after about a year. Then Roberts left and Sheasby took over, to be joined by his son Thomas Jnr.

The Swansea Canal was completed in July 1798 and, very unusually, the job had been brought in under its £60,000 budget. This was a fine achievement considering that there were many major works involved. The succession of valleys to the west, each with its own river, made sure that a number of aqueducts were needed.

One – over the Afon Twrch – at Gurnos is a fine three-arched structure. It is also scheduled as an Ancient Monument and was the scene of the first application of "hydraulic cement" as a canal bed lining, rather than the then normal method of sealing with clay puddling. This was a mixture that, when applied, sealed the bed of the canal, drying out even under water.

Locks were the other major task. It needed 36 of them to lift the canal to its summit level some 373 feet (113.7m) above sea level. They took boats of 69ft by 7ft 7ins (20.9m x 2.3m) which could carry up to 25 tonnes.

Additionally, there were small branch canals – arms really, and mainly built privately. The ironworks at Ynysgedwyn and Ystalyfera both had one – the eighteenth century equivalent of having a private railway siding.

And, being Wales, there were tramways. One huge undertaking was the Brecon Forest Tramroad. Originally, this ran to Castell-du, on the edge of Sennybridge, from the lime quarries at Penwyllt. This actually had no connection with the Swansea canal in its early days in that its main purpose was to carry traffic north, away from the canal. In their original dreams, the canal promoters had hoped to reach Sennybridge, but this had clearly been an impractical scheme.

After several years of acute financial instability, including the bankruptcy of its original owner and builder, a connection was made southwards and the tramroad reached the canal around 1833. It was short-lived. Records surviving show the minuscule receipts from this 19 mile (30.6km) line could never have made it anything but a drain on its owner's purse. It must be regarded as a less than shrewd investment, and never really contributed much to the wealth of the canal itself.

A massive stone aqueduct carried the Swansea Canal over Afon Twrch at Gurnos.

Other – shorter – tramroads ran off up each of the valleys on the west side of the canal. To the east, several crossed the river on flimsy bridges to bring their raw materials to this wonderful new transport artery. Collieries, often only a few hundred yards away from the water installed tramroads to gain full benefit from the canal.

One minor claim that the Swansea Canal has to a smidgen of fame is that it carried the very first iron manufactured by a new process that dramatically improved quality whilst reducing manufacturing costs.

In Ynys-Cedwyn Ironworks, near Gurnos, a young man – one David Thomas – was employed. Starting there in 1817, he became absorbed by a conundrum that was taxing other brains at the time. Coal used in the iron smelting process had to be of a bituminous type not available locally. But there was anthracite all around, albeit unsuitable to the task in hand.

By 1824, Thomas was experimenting to find ways of improving combustibility of fuel. He met with only limited success for a time, but eventually came up with a method of producing a hot blast that would work with anthracite. The works owner agreed to convert a furnace specially for the job in 1837, to great success. Not that blast furnaces in themselves were new. The first recorded in the world was in China in 28BC.

News of his achievement spread overseas and he was head-hunted by a company in Pennsylvania USA. They were involved in ironmaking, also owning extensive anthracite mines.

He emigrated with his family in 1839 and became very successful, soon owning his own iron-making company over there. By 1864, the process was being pursued to such effect that the country was producing more iron than Wales. An early example of the brain-drain, Thomas died a wealthy man in 1882, having reached the ripe old age of 88.

Few records remain detailing the volume of traffic this canal carried. One thing is certain: there was lots. Congestion around Swansea was a fact. The dock was a heaving mass of boats and an urgently-needed new dock was proposed by 1830.

This seemed to come to nothing, because it was 1852 before North Dock was finally opened. But railway competition was, by now, in the air. The first line from Swansea had been opened up the Tawe valley to coal mines at Graig Ola. This was mainly along level ground, and did not overtax the railway engineers. But the steep valley ahead did not daunt them for long either.

Within nine years, the iron road had reached Ystradgynlais, using a route along the east side of the valley. This had an immediate and devastating effect on the canal's traffic from that side: it virtually disappeared.

Not that this had a remarkable effect on the canal's profit, so firmly based was the rest of the trade. By the early nineteenth century, investors were starting to take a dividend. By 1810, this was into double figures and there it stayed, almost unbroken, for over fifty years. In the heady days of the mid 1850s, the Lord Mayor's Show decade before the refuse cart of the 1860s and beyond, up to 18% was being paid. A handsome return indeed.

Alterations to the canal's layout around Swansea were undertaken with the opening of North Dock. But, by the early 1860s, things were starting to look less chromium-plated for both owners and traders.

Steel – as mentioned in Chapter Five – was starting to replace iron. The country was in the grip of a recession: not a twentieth-century phenomenon after all, only the name then was different. Railways were nibbling away at trade. The canals, being in a far stronger position financially than the newcomers, were able to offer a reduction in tolls. That saw some of the traffic that had wandered away returning, and receipts started to climb again by the end of that decade.

Learning from their counterparts on other canals, the company started to look around for a railway company to take a lease on their assets. The Great Western Railway ended up with the business, but paid far more than was usual at the time – January 1873.

The reason was simple competition. The GWR in this instance did not have a monopoly of rail traffic in the area. The Midland, strangely, had a finger into Wales here and threatened the GWR's trade. Accordingly, the canal was not bled dry in that company's normal way, but was worked intensively and efficiently.

But the inevitable could not be deferred for long. By the mid 1880s, the two major iron producers had closed. Their production – as well as incoming raw materials – was lost. Despite this, the canal still managed to carry over 385,000 tonnes in 1888 and did not actually start to lose money until 1895. By this time, the top section had been completely abandoned.

A similar fate overtook most of the rest by the early years of the twentieth century, but the lowest six miles continued to carry substantial freight until after the Great War.

One "trade", of which there is still much documentation, was the use of boats for social outings. Whitsun celebrations, so beloved of the Methodist church, were a time of great festivities and sports. Often, fields arranged to accommodate the events were canalside and part of the fun was a trip along the canal to get there.

For this, working boats were meticulously cleaned so that children's (and ladies) best clothes would not make contact with the grime normally associated with these craft. That was of crucial importance – almost more so than any other consideration. Don't forget that in the early part of this century, the words "Sunday Best" meant just that. Poverty was such that there was a severe limit to the amount of clothing anyone possessed, and "Whit Wear" was even more special: Sunday clothes augmented with something new. Definitely not the attire that could bear contact with coal dust or any other detritus.

An old lock chamber at Godre'r-Graig has been incorporated into a garden.

These trips – wonderful community events, now sadly only a memory – lasted on the canal right up to the start of the last war.

A number of Acts were needed to close the canal completely, the final one by the British Transport Commission in 1962.

And Now ...

If you are the type who likes a challenge, the Swansea Canal presents as much fun as any in Wales. With diligent application and common sense, there are endless bits of the old line that can be detected. And "detected" is the word.

Clues are all around. The contours of the land, a little bit of ancient masonry alongside a busy road, a line of mature trees – even street and house names; all must be in your armoury if this fascinating game is to be played well.

Starting in Swansea is pretty much a waste of time. All the factories have long since gone and the course of the canal is infilled. But, a depression in the ground here, a regular mound there, and it is possible to piece together the route.

The canal ran up the Tawe valley. Follow the A4067 from town towards junction 45 on the M4. At this island, take the B4603 towards Clydach. On the right almost a mile (1.6km) along at SN 683005 a macadamed path leads off. This soon picks up the route of the canal, but, at this point, there is no sign of it.

This closes in on the river for a short distance before heading past a storage compound on the left, across Station Road and along another lane beside a scrap yard and past Angie's Cafe, following a Public Footpath sign. This is now detectable as a canal course, a fact that is soon confirmed as water appears. Already the towing path is good, and will remain so for the entire watered section.

After only a few yards, a treasure. This aqueduct takes the canal over the Lower Clydach river in great style. There is a pleasant view from here and the whole area is quite attractive.

Clydach High Street bridge has been lowered, meaning a road crossing and immediately past another lock. Ahead, an obstruction: a builder's yard. The canal is piped under here whilst the towing path passes to the left hand side of the yard between two brick walls.

The canal passes under Pontardawe Road with the Coed Gwilym Centre and Park on the right. During the season, canoes and dinghies can be hired here. A plaque notes that this length of canal was opened

The old iron works at Ynys-Cedwyn used to be served by a canal arm.

for leisure use on May 20th 1981. After the park there is a golf course on the right. As there are some balls to be seen in the canal, it is not unreasonable to assume that a mighty slice from some hapless golfer will produce a flying missile that would be quite detrimental to health should it be stopped by a head: watch out!

There is a ruined lock along this section followed by a pretty bridge that started out as a stone one but has been "improved" and widened with brick. A few yards to the left of this bridge is a pub called The Colliers Arms. Above the bridge, another ruined lock with the collar and anchor straps of the bottom gates still clearly visible.

The canal is now cut into the hillside with housing to the left and a bosky slope on the right, often falling steeply down to the Tawe which accompanies the canal for much of this section. A water course enters the canal from the left, and is relieved almost at once by a spillway under the towing path.

Then the water ends and ahead, a vast area of playing fields. Follow the private road which is (more or less) on the line of the canal to a supermarket car park. In the top left hand corner is a subway under the main road. At the end, the canal is again in water. The locks here disappeared under the new road. An aqueduct crosses the Upper Clydach River. Flattened road-bridges litter the passage through Pontardawe. There is a pretty garden canalside with a red asphalt path; much effort has been expended here to make it attractive.

A trip boat will be found moored by Foundry Wharf. Operated by the Canal Society, it offers the chance of a short cruise on the canal during the summer. Details at the end of this chapter.

The Swansea Canal Society operate a trip boat at Pontardawe.

Still heading generally north, the Swansea Canal enters a more open area. The remains of the half mile (800m) Cilybebyll Arm which served collieries on the other side of the valley. Two more locks bring the canal to a flattened crossing at Ynysmeudwy. A pub is located a few yards to the left.

Then starts the final watered section. One mile (1.6km) long, it curves gently right, past the remains of a lock, before reaching the main road. From here, the dewatered course is easily followed as the ground starts to rise, gently at first, then more steeply. This section was punctuated by locks as the canal staggered up the hill.

Towards the top, the course disappears under the road, but at the brow of the hill, the left hand wall of the top lock has been retained and amalgamated into a garden; to great effect. Bear left, along the footpath and follow the canal's bed. The valley widens here somewhat. Over to the right, steep hills are unblemished by trees, whilst to the left, a few houses cling precariously to the sheer sides: magnificent.

This lasts for about half a mile (800m) and then the course moves to the right, but the path does not. After reaching a road, take the first opportunity to turn right, cross the main road (not by the subway) and walk along the right hand side towards a tarred path. This, again, is the course of the canal, and leads to the spectacular three-arched aqueduct over the river Twrch at Gurnos (SN 773093).

Beyond the aqueduct, it is possible to gauge the route past the Aubrey Arms, across the road and into the trees. There is a new technology park on the right and immediately beyond the entrance to this is an unmarked lane to the left. This leads to a farm and a house, and there is evidence of the canal on the left for almost three hundred yards, but no road exit from the lane. Walkers can turn left and at the main road, right and up to the next road on the right. Drivers return to the main A4067, turn right and some 700 yards (640m) along, on the right, is a road.

At this point (SN 778098) the Ynys-Cedwyn arm joined the main canal. This ½ mile (800m) arm, privately owned, linked the canal with the eponymous iron works. This is the place where David Thomas carried out his experiments, and there is evidence of iron being worked there in 1612. It finished casting iron in 1876 although tin was then made here until final closure in 1941.

Today, some of the original building remains, preserved by the local council. The framework of a building and accompanying chimney are clear to see. Also at this junction, the Brecon Forest Tramway joined the canal. The route this followed can be gauged by the line of the road.

To explore this canal arm, follow the Public Footpath sign to the right of the junction. This follows a tarmac path with the depression that was the canal to the right. At some stage, cross to the right hand bank as, soon, a couple of new houses will force the left hand path away from the water. Past these, there is occasional evidence of masonry on the far bank. The line ends at a road haulage yard. Turn left with the path, right at the road and the ironworks is a few yards along on the left. Retrace your steps back to the main line.

Heading along the main line again, beyond this point, traces of the canal's existence become scant. The main road, by-passing Ystradgynlais, uses the same narrow corridor along the side of the valley. There is some evidence; again, detective skills must be to the fore. Lock Cottage is one, to the right at the far end (SN 799115), just before a traffic island.

Here, a Public Footpath sign points the route of the canal, away to the left. This leads along what was clearly the course and arrives at The Castle pub (currently closed). Ahead is a track, but it is on private land.

Cross the flattened canal bridge and follow the road which runs alongside the course and to the left. At the next road turn right, back over the course. On the left, just above the road, are the remains of another lock.

Turn left at the main road. The course now closely follows the road, although the bed is dry. A little further up, on the left at SN 806124 is some evidence of a bridge. There is a broken cast iron notice here concerning rights of way. The canal probably crossed the road here, judging by the sweep of the trees further up on the right.

And that is it. The terminal basin lay behind the Rheolau Arms pub on the left (SN 811126), but has become overgrown and put to other uses.

One connection with the great age of ironmaking in the Tawe valley is still to be seen today. The trip boat operated by the Swansea Canal Society. Named DAVID "PAPA" THOMAS after the inventor of anthracite iron-production mentioned earlier.

Clydach Aqueduct, Swansea Canal.

Maps

Landranger sheets 159, 160 and 170 cover the whole canal. The *A to Z Swansea Street Atlas*, published by Geographer's Map Co. Ltd. details the line from Swansea to Ynysmeudwy at 4 miles to the inch (1 : 15840).

Public Transport

Swansea buses cover all the route, but with a whole range of different services. Most useful for the lower section is South Wales Transport service 120 which operates between Swansea, Clydach, Pontardawe, Ynysmeudwy and Ystalyfera every day including Sundays. Ring the Enquiry Line on 01792 580580 for full details.

Societies

The Swansea Canal Society exists to promote the existence of the canal. They organise working parties and operate the trip boat from Pontardawe. Their secretary is Clive Reed, 34, Ynysmeudwy Road, Ynysmeudwy, Pontardawe, Swansea SA8 4QD – 01792 864637.

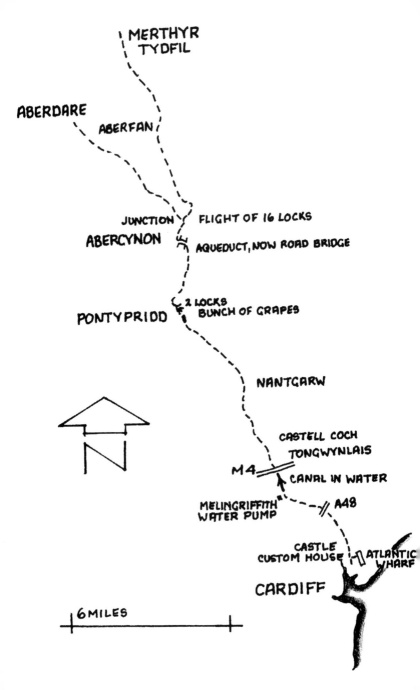

9. The Aberdare Canal

Then ...

In terms of gestation, the Aberdare Canal was one of the longest in Wales. The original Act was granted in 1793, but boats were not seen on it until 1812.

The reason for this inordinate delay on such a small undertaking was the company's desire to concentrate on tramroads. Hirwaun already had some of these, and the thinking was to tap into the ironworks trade in this area and bring it down to Aberdare to a site where the canal basin would be built. Whether this was an acute case of cart-before-the-horse is not clear.

It is, however, crystal clear that times were hard. Many of the investors were financially committed to the Glamorganshire and that company was making continued calls upon its shareholders.

Strangely, the tramway actually made a small profit – by carrying coal AWAY from the canal. The ironworks in Hirwaun already had a source of limestone to the north of Penderyn and this was delivered along a tramway. The Aberdare company's tramway now provided good transport for coal.

And there matters rested, but not for long. The Aberdare Ironworks, a large undertaking for its time, opened in Llwydcoed, just above Aberdare. The Neath Canal (see Chapter Four) were arranging to have a tramroad built to link Hirwaun with their water. The Aberdare Iron Company were keen to have some form of efficient transport and their company was duly serviced by this line.

The canal company looked at many other ideas for tramroads; in fact, they appeared to be most reluctant to build the actual canal that had inspired the original Bill. But many of the original committee had sold their interests in the company and new blood was coming in. These were mainly businessmen from the Afon Cynon and included John Scale, one of the owners of the Aberdare Ironworks.

Another survey was commissioned in 1809 and Thomas Sheasby Jnr. appointed as Engineer. He did not last very long. A "better offer" saw him decamp. Construction continued with George Overton appointed in 1811. In 1812, the first boats started to move. The waterway had not reached the Aberdare Ironworks, but a tramway had been laid connecting the two.

The canal was constructed to the same nominal size as the Glamorganshire, 60ft by 8ft 9ins (18.2m x 2.5m). It was a little short of 7 miles (11km), ran from Aberdare to join the Glamorganshire at Abercynon and needed only two locks; strange, considering the very hilly nature of the terrain. There was also a stop lock where it joined the Glamorganshire.

These locks are essentially a water conservation measure. When a new canal wanted to join an existing one, the former usually insisted that the newcomer was built on a slightly higher level. Often with a fall of only a few inches, the stop lock ensured that the old company not only did not lose water to the newcomer, but actually gained a little each time a boat moved. Water was a valuable commodity, even two centuries ago.

Because of the delay in opening, the Aberdare missed out on a lot of traffic. Bankruptcy had struck the main works in Hirwaun, and many of those remaining continued to use the Neath. Trade on the canal was disappointing.

Then, revolution. Enter the Seventh Cavalry in the shape of the Crawshays whom we have met on other canals in Wales. In 1819 they took over the Hirwaun works. Dynamism ruled then. They bought shares in the canal, applied an elegant leather boot to its posterior by cutting all tolls by half and soon started on a number of improvements to the line that would increase the carrying capacity of the boats.

That the concern benefited from enlightened management is beyond doubt. What was still a problem was the lack of traffic: it just wasn't there.

As the years passed, further businesses were opened in the valley. Trade continued, and being such an efficiently run organisation, there was a profit. But the best days were still ahead.

In 1838, some 60,000 tonnes of freight moved along the Aberdare, almost the same as a decade earlier. But coal was beginning to make its presence felt, particularly steam coal. Collieries were being sunk all along the valley as the rich seams were tapped. In fact, trade boomed to such an extent that water supply then became a problem and a pump had to be built in 1846 to add water from the Cynon.

Another ten years along and the tonnages had almost trebled, although the proprietors were not laughing all the way to the bank: railways had arrived. Afon Cynon was under attack from both ends. The Vale of Neath line came in via Hirwaun whilst the Taff Vale had made its way up the valley from Abercynon.

However, despite this competition, the canal continued to flourish. There was simply too much coal to be moved and it needed both rail and canal working at full stretch to cope. 1858 was reached and the tonnage carried had risen to a staggering 220,000 tonnes.

It could not last, and it didn't. Another decade along and the figures had more than halved. Carriage rates had also fallen so that by 1875 alarming noises about the future were being heard. In 1885, Lord Bute, having taken over the Glamorganshire, also assumed control of the Aberdare.

By this time, the source of so much trade – coal – had started to have an adverse effect on the integrity of the canal itself. Subsidence was becoming a problem and navigation was increasingly difficult. By 1898 there was no iron or coal carried, just a small tonnage of sundries and closure was decided upon in 1900.

An Act of 1924 closed the canal legally and transferred ownership of most of the line to local councils. The Aberdare was not required as a water course, and much of it has been infilled over the years.

And Now ...

The bed of the canal was in a prime position for the council's road improvers to use. And they did. The main A4059 along the Cynon valley used much of the canal as increased vehicular traffic demanded ever more space.

Which leaves little for today's explorer to discover. It is almost as though this vital trade artery had never existed. Alongside the road there are a few lengths of wall which indicate where the canal ran, but effectively, a trip to Aberdare is a frustrating experience. Only your own detective skills can reveal what lies hidden.

Maps

The whole of the canal's route is on Ordnance Survey Sheet 170. An older 1: 25,000 scale gives some indication of the route.

Public Transport

Regional Railways service from Cardiff to Aberdare travels the same valley as the canal from Abercynon.

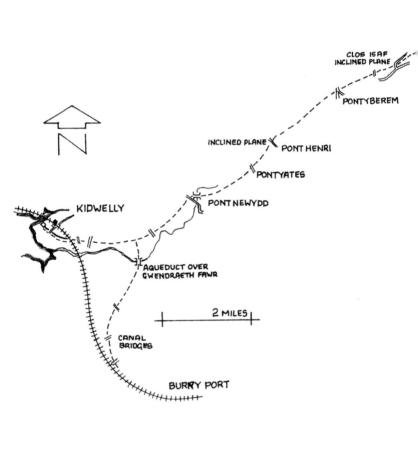

CLOS ISAF
INCLINED PLANE

PONTYBEREM

INCLINED PLANE

PONT HENRI

PONTYATES

KIDWELLY

PONT NEWYDD

AQUEDUCT OVER
GWENDRAETH FAWR

2 MILES

CANAL
BRIDGES

BURRY PORT

10. The Kidwelly & Llanelli Canal

Then ...

A total misnomer: the canal never got anywhere near Llanelli. It was also a mish-mash of other projects that actually started with the first canal in Wales, Kymer's.

This was a 3 mile (4.8km) canal along the Gwendraeth Fawr valley from coal and limestone workings near Carway down to Kidwelly. It ran independently of the river and finished at a quay in the town. Authorised in 1766, it was built lock-free, opening in 1769.

A completely separate company proposed extending the canal further up the river towards the rich anthracite fields around Pantyffynnon. Whilst this came to nothing, the idea never really died. Further proposals saw an Act being granted to the Kidwelly and Llanelli Canal and Tramroad Company in 1812. This authorised a canal from the head of Kymer's Canal to Pontyberem. From there, a tramroad would reach further up the valley to Cwm-mawr. Two members of the Kymer family were amongst the initial investors.

There was to be a further branch from below Spuddersbridge, near Llandyry, to Llanelli. This would service a number of collieries en route, including those belonging to the Earl of Ashburnham who had built a 1½ mile (2.4km) canal himself around 1796.

The engineer appointed was James Pinkerton. Work got off to a fine start but, before long, funds began to run low. The estimate for the job had been way out. Work staggered to a halt around 1816 after making a junction with the Earl of Ashburnham's canal at Ffrwd. Some work was done on the northern extension which included construction of two locks.

And there things stood until 1825. Then, the Pembrey New Harbour Company was formed. Their purpose was to build what we know today as Burry Port, complete with a short connection to the K & L. That was complete by 1832, but there was no canal to connect into. Enter James Green.

With his almost pathological hatred of locks, Green set about surveying what was needed. He reported that in his opinion the canal should be continued eastward to Burry Port. From there, a tramroad should link the end of the canal with another – the already extant Pembrey Canal – at Pwll. As for the Gwendraeth Fawr line, that was to be extended for another 5 miles (8km) by means of three inclined planes.

Inclined planes were Green's favoured method of overcoming hills. Essentially, they were built as a slope up a hillside with guide rails. Boats very different to the standard were employed. These were known as tub boats and were just that, looking like tubs. Carrying some 6 tonnes, they measured roughly 20 feet by 6 feet 4 ins and were some 2 feet 6 ins deep (6.1m x 1.9m x .45m),* with wheels on the bottom.

They were towed along by horses in trains of up to 6. On reaching a plane, the tubs were hooked to a rope and pulled up (or lowered) to the next level. The motive power for this was often a waterwheel, but evidence suggests that on this canal, two pairs of rails were provided. This indicates that gravity was the prime moving force. Tubs would be hooked on, one at the top, another at the bottom. The descending one would pull up the ascending one.

Larger – more standard – boats were used lower down the canal. Whether the tubs were worked throughout their journey or trans-shipping was involved, we have no records.

These development proposals were put to a company meeting, approved, and work was started in 1834. To what extent the work was completed is not fully documented. By 1830, the Burry Port extension was finished, and as much of the valley line as ever got built. The canal never actually reached the harbour, stopping some four hundred yards

---

These measurements are very approximate, based on Green's general standard on other canals. No records of his K & L tubs survive.

(360m) short and being linked to the quays by tramway.

Starting at Pontyates – where the original construction work had finished – Green built two locks to Ponthenri. Inclined planes both there and at Capel Ifan were completed and working. There is no evidence to show that the third, scheduled for Hirwaun-isaf, was ever completed. A water channel was dug to Cwm-mawr, but it was not believed to be navigable. A tramway ran alongside. Green, meanwhile, had been dismissed. His inability to complete the planes within budget saw him replaced.

By this time, the real boom in canals elsewhere was already at an end. Railways were making their presence felt, and would soon do likewise in this far-flung part of the canal network.

Much of the anthracite was now being shipped through Burry Port. Kidwelly had never been an ideal spot, suffering from shoaling and difficult access. The construction of better facilities at Burry Port hastened this decline.

Overall, tonnages were minuscule when compared to other canals considered between these covers. 57,000 tonnes seems to be the highest figure recorded; that in 1863. Soon after, railway interlopers were making their presence felt. Anxious not to lose income, the company transmogrified into The Kidwelly and Burry Port Railway Company. They obtained an Act allowing them to close the canal and build a railway in its place.

This was duly effected. But before any firm action was taken, an amalgamation with the Burry Port harbour owners was deemed a sound financial move, thus to maintain their pre-eminence in the export of coal. This final move also included a name change. Now the organisation · was known as the Burry Port and Gwendraeth Valley Railway.

The first to be converted was the valley route to Pontyberem which was completed in 1869. As this used some of the canal bed, navigation finished some time before that date. The exact closure is not recorded, but 1867 would seem to be a pretty accurate assessment.

Thus, the very short life of the Kidwelly and Llanelli as a canal came to an end.

And Now ...

Seeking out what remains of this canal can be a very frustrating experience. What does remain is pretty fragmented and makes a road exploration the only way to achieve anything, except for one length.

This is below Kidwelly. Here, a length of the canal by the old harbour is complete and in water. Turn off the A484 in Kidwelly at Station Road. At the end, turn left over the level crossing and where the road forks take the left, past the sewage works to a bridge over the canal at SN 399062. There is ample parking space here.

Turn right along the path which leads towards the harbour. Left, a pleasant stroll of some 400 yards (380m) brings the canal to an end by the main railway line. There is a path on the other bank, so it is possible to walk back by a slightly different route.

Elsewhere, as previously noted, the railway was built on the line of the canal. The aqueduct over Gwendraeth Fawr at SN 427053 was also converted for rail use, but is on private land.

Of the remainder of the line to Burry Port, there is hardly any certain sign. Up the valley, marshy ground by the railway bridge in Pontnewydd (SN 447073) gives no more than an indication of the course. In Ponthenri, at SN 4770094, a pub called The Incline (free house) marks the top of that inclined plane. The slope is still evident, as it is at Closisaf (SN 522121, The incline, to the east of the railway, although now heavily wooded, is plain to see.

And that's about it. Sad. Although it was not one of Wales' most famous canals, the K & L was so different from the rest. It would have been a real delight had any of the equipment survived and would have added immeasurably to our knowledge of canals.

Maps

Ordnance Survey sheet 159 covers all the canal and its branches.

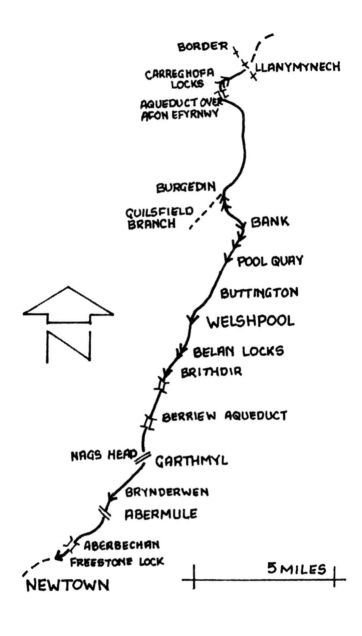

BORDER

CARREGHOFA
LOCKS

LLANYMYNECH

AQUEDUCT OVER
AFON EFYRNWY

BURGEDIN

QUILSFIELD
BRANCH

BANK

POOL QUAY

BUTTINGTON

WELSHPOOL

BELAN LOCKS

BRITHDIR

BERRIEW AQUEDUCT

NAGS HEAD

GARTHMYL

BRYNDERWEN

ABERMULE

ABERBECHAN

FREESTONE LOCK

NEWTOWN

5 MILES

11. The Montgomeryshire Canal

The history of this very rural canal in inextricably linked with the Ellesmere – see Chapter Twelve. For that reason, the pre-history to this proposal is dealt with there, only the construction is considered now.

Canal mania was at its height by the early 1790s and any town with the slightest pretension to being forward looking wanted to be included in proposals. With the Ellesmere Canal being planned to Llanymynech, the proposal was to drive a canal north from Welshpool to meet it. Further proposals to head south to Newtown were soon added and it was this package that was presented to Parliament. An Act was granted in March 1794 for a canal from Porth-y-waen, north of Llanymynech to Newtown.

It was recognised at the outset that with little bulk industry to support it, the company would be hard pressed to make their living from agricultural produce. Thus, the people who invested did so for more altruistic motives. They were mainly noblemen and others who lived in the area and could afford some largesse.

The brothers Dadford – John and Thomas Jnr. – were appointed joint engineers and started work on the 23½ mile (37.8km) line. 13 locks were needed. Unusually, the ends of the canal start at a high level, each descending to a valley near Burgedin. On most canals, the gradient rises from each end to meet on a summit level.

There were several difficulties encountered during the construction. Principal of these were aqueducts. The canal ran generally along the western side of the Severn valley, and each of that river's tributaries had to be crossed.

Unusual iron and brick bridge over the Montgomeryshire Canal at Glanhafren.

Work was soon under way and proceeded apace. By August 1797, the canal had made its link with the Ellesmere at Carreghofa and reached Garthmyl, just 7 miles from Newtown. A 2¼ mile (3.6km) branch to Guilsfield in the west from the main line at Burgedin was also completed around this time. The original proposal to reach Porth-y-waen was never achieved, and the company remained satisfied with their canal as it was. The quarries at the northern end, the original motive for the canal, eventually reached the waterside by means of a tramway.

And there matters lay: the money had run out. John Dadford had left the team, to be replaced by his father. Surprisingly, trade was at a higher level than had been forecast. This was in part due to the war. Cereal crops were fetching a very high price, and farmers were doing all they could to increase production.

This meant lime on the land. That commodity was available in abundance around Llanymynech and many kilns were built alongside the canal to burn it. This needed coal of course, and a trade in that commodity helped keep the carriage tolls coming in.

But the "peace dividend" was not a financial one for those concerned with the canal. Trade in limestone and coal halved as the slump took hold. This was not greatly felt in Newtown. Business and consequently population was starting to thrive. The idea of continuing the canal was floated, and a complicated series of financial manoeuvres then took place.

The canal company owners, still enjoying an unexpected dividend on their shares, even if reduced somewhat from previous years, were reluctant to see it disappear into the hole that a new canal would become. A tramway was proposed as a cheaper option, but eventually discarded. So keen were they to avoid the extension that the proprietors actively opposed the new Act that would be needed.

It took two years of negotiations before an accommodation could be reached. This involved the establishment of what amounted to a separate company to build and operate the line. This was to become known as the Western Branch. John Williams was the engineer, although Josias Jessup, son of the famous William, carried out the detailed survey. A Bill was presented and the Act granted in 1815.

Construction under way, there were no real engineering problems to be overcome on the 7½ mile (12km) length. Six locks were needed, together with a water supply which came from the Severn just north of Newtown.

The canal was reported as built by 1819, but another contemporary source states that it was not completed until 1821. Whatever, the financial wrangling continued as initial revenues were even less than predicted. Conflicting factions fought a long and bitter battle to establish their respective vision of financial probity.

By 1835, the Western company were well enough organised to pay a small dividend. Not that these problems affected the Eastern company. Their trade continued to be good. Passenger flyboats were introduced in 1836. These were "fliers", almost in the literal sense, and ran from Newtown all the way to London.

Flyboats had absolute priority over other craft. Others got out of the way – for one very good reason. If they did not, their towlines would be cut by the flyboat crew. They worked continually throughout the twenty four hours with two crews, one working, one resting. Fresh horses were provided in relays along the route.

Freight trade continued to improve along both sections of the canal until a recession took hold in 1840. This lasted for nearly five years before things started to pick up again, but by then, railways were starting to explore the area.

In 1845, the canal committee decided to examine the possibility of changing their operation into a railway, but events elsewhere were overtaking them. They were approached by the Shropshire Union Canal Company directors in 1846 with a view to selling out to this new enterprise. The Eastern committee accepted, and on Friday January 1st 1847, the SUC took over.

The Western section remained independent, continuing to maintain a good level of trade. However, the inevitable could not be deferred for too long, and on Tuesday February 5th 1850, they also became a part of the SUC. The full history of the Shropshire Union Canal will be found in Chapter Twelve.

As part of this new conglomerate, the Montgomeryshire became something of a backwater, especially as the SUC soon leased themselves to the London and North Western Railway Company.

By 1861, a rival company had opened a railway directly competing with the Montgomery line. To say that this had a deleterious effect on trade is something of an understatement, but the LNWR, unlike the GWR whose depredations have been discussed earlier, made some efforts to retain trade.

Under the railway grouping of 1923, the LNWR became a part of the London Midland and Scottish Railway. Their view of canal carrying was much more in tune with GWR ideas. They looked at trade on their canals, and didn't like what they saw.

Only 9,000 tonnes of freight moved the year they took over. During the next decade, most of this trade disappeared. A flannel mill in Newtown closed in 1935, and another 400 tonnes a year went.

Old warehouse alongside the Montgomery Canal at Brynderwen, Glanhafren.

On February 5th 1936, the Ellesmere Branch breached, about a mile below the junction at Frankton. The exact point is at SJ 366306. This effectively cut off the Montgomeryshire Canal from the rest of the system.

Faced with a potential bill for £16,000, the company offered compensation to the only carrier left on the canal and applied for a closure warrant. This was refused, and the LMS were instructed to apply for an Act. This they did in 1944, when the Montgomeryshire was closed along with most of the rest of the Shropshire Union system. Details of this infamous deed will be found in Chapter Twelve.

With the granting of this Act, all rights to navigation were extinguished and local councils left free to alter bridges as they saw necessary. It became County highway policy to flatten these in the interests of road safety. This continued until the late 1960s when the possibility of restoration was first mooted.

By this time, all but one of the nine bridges that carry the A483 over the canal during its journey from Llanganydr south had gone, together with many others carrying lesser roads. Since that nadir, the outlook has improved immeasurably, and full restoration is now considered only a matter of time.

First murmurings were noted in 1968 when the Shropshire Union Canal Society started to take an interest in one of the constituent parts of the SUC. From their initial interest, an embryonic Preservation Group was established. Their first task was to persuade those local authorities through whose territory the line passed, that restoration was a feasible proposition.

This in itself was no easy task. As the 1960s ended and the new decade dawned, initial scepticism was slowly worn away, and the attitude moved right through to enthusiastic co-operation. Then came the masterstroke: the Prince of Wales became interested. This raised the profile immeasurably and was perhaps the greatest single catalyst to the current situation.

The first section to be restored was north of Welshpool. This was chosen because of its high visibility as a project, and the relative simplicity of the task. The £300,000 needed for this was raised by the Prince of Wales Committee. With that work complete, the ladies of the Inland Waterways Association raised money to provide a boat adapted for use by the handicapped.

Again, the "Monty" led the way. The HEULWEN/SUNSHINE became the first ever canal boat specifically equipped. To this day, she ploughs her watery furrow along the canal, giving joy, relaxation and relief to thousands of people, all ages and both sexes.

As the eighties dawned, it became clear that almost total restoration was feasible. Only the most southerly 1½ miles outside Newtown was excluded, some of this section having been built upon. The faith of a few devotees in their cause would soon be justified.

The whole business of restoration was placed on a formal footing by the formation of The Montgomery Waterway Restoration Trust. All the local authorities and voluntary bodies were involved along with British Waterways. But there then occurred a major problem. A submission had been made to the Secretary of State for Wales – then Peter Walker –

for a package of full funding via an application to the EC. It seemed a formality, until he refused to forward the request. The expected accessibility to funds for full restoration suddenly disappeared.

Everyone was bewildered, but not for long. Although legally abandoned, British Waterways had already put in train the necessary steps to obtain parliamentary approval for the canal – a vital move that would allow them to spend money on it. A new Act was granted in 1987, and the restoration seemed "on" again.

But other potential problems were to present themselves. Conservation was one huge stumbling block. As they fall into disuse, canals tend to become a refuge for a wide range of flora and fauna, and any prospect of disturbance to their habitat is viewed with concern by conservationists. This fear is recognised, and can be backed up by a declaration from the Nature Conservancy Council that an area is a Site of Special Scientific Interest. Once declared, activity within the area defined is strictly controlled. Much of the "Monty" is so declared.

There has long been a conflict between naturalists who want to preserve things the way they are, and those who want to open up these former waterways for the benefit of anglers, walkers and boaters. In recent years, this has been taken to extremes on the Basingstoke Canal in Surrey and Hampshire, and the Pocklington Canal in Yorkshire.

The latter caused a huge outcry within the boating world. In the 1960s, a small group of canal enthusiasts fought a long and hard battle against local authority plans to infill the redundant waterway. They won, and started restoration. But, having saved the canal from the planners, their dream of a waterway complete with boats and anglers came to an abrupt end.

Someone discovered a rare plant in the water, a SSSI was proclaimed, and all work came to a halt. That this newly-discovered oasis would have already gone but for the boaters weighed not in the balance of fair play, and the situation is still only partially resolved after long and tedious discussions.

Anxious to avoid this problem on the "Monty", restorers have worked with the Nature Conservancy Council. This has resulted in the creation of seventeen off-line reserves where rarer forms of life are to be transferred. This was particularly the case when floating water plantain was discovered in the canal. One of the world's rarest plants, it was duly moved to a reserve where it can continue to flourish.

A House of Commons Select Committee was formed in 1988 to examine the Montgomeryshire project. Their decision that the canal should be restored in full saw the plans hitting top gear again. Sadly, no positive access to funds was mentioned. Since then, it has been a case of making haste slowly.

And Now ...

After half a century of dereliction, the Montgomeryshire Canal is well on its way to becoming a living thing again. Most of the major restoration is actually taking place on the old Ellesmere section, and thus not within the scope of this book. The whole venture, excluding the last short section into Newtown, is projected for completion early in the twenty-first century.

Some work is currently being carried out along various lengths of the Montgomery, both east and west. Because this is a process that will inevitably accelerate, much of the condition of this waterway as reported between these pages will alter in due course. What will not change is the spectacular beauty of its surroundings. Perhaps not quite so dramatic as the more intimate valley canals in the south, but the broad trough that is the Severn valley makes for much more expansive views.

The finest way to explore is on foot with the whole length available to walkers – including virtually all the abandoned length near Newtown. Although not actually a legal right of way, the towing path is there, available, and walking is actively encouraged.

The full 23½ miles (37.8km) may be a little too much to tackle at one go, but there is public transport available to allow one way walking. One bus virtually mirrors the canal by travelling along the A483. Full details are at the foot of this chapter.

At Carreghofa locks (SJ 255203) the small creek on the far bank above the locks is the water supply, provided by the river Tanat. The two locks

Aberbechan Kiln Bridge, Montgomery Canal.

here are exquisitely restored, the houses covered in Virginia Creeper and the whole effect is absolutely charming. The work was carried out by the Shropshire Union Canal Society, and reflects great credit on them.

Also worthy of note at these locks is a fine example of the unique paddle gear used to let water into the locks. On most canals, this is achieved by a simple vertical paddle which covered a culvert. Using rack and pinion – often geared – this paddle was lifted to allow in the water. It can be seen on the bottom gates on the canal.

On the Montgomeryshire, the top paddles moved in the horizontal. Made for the company at Coalbrookdale, some have since been replaced by standard gear. This is a fine example of one aspect of the individuality which so distinguished earlier canals.

A few hundred yards along, another flattened bridge leads to a short remote section before reaching one of the most dramatic lengths of this canal. The aqueduct over the Afon Efyrnwy (SJ 254196) is simply stunning. Long, and very narrow, it strides boldly across the wide river bed reaching towards Four Crosses, where refreshment and shops are available. This is also the site of the first major canal settlement on the

Monty. Here, there was a wharf, warehouse and four lime kilns.

• Leave the canal and head left for 200 yards (183m).

The scenery becomes increasingly breathtaking, and steeply rising hills make their presence felt. The canal will weave quite wildly over the next mile or so, attempting – and succeeding – to hold the contour. As it does so, there are two crossings of the main road, both flattened.

The two Burgedin Locks (SJ 252146) are reached next, with an arm leaving to the right. This was the Guilsfield Branch. Some of it can still be traced, preserved as a nature reserve, but the majority has now disappeared.

These locks are the last "downhill" ones as the canal reaches a valley and the excess water runs into the river Severn by the New Cut. The canal has fallen 32 feet 2 inches (9.7m) thus far. By the first bridge, a slipway has been provided near Wern (SJ 251136). 1½ miles (2.4km) beyond, four restored locks – Bank, Cabin, Crowther Hall and Pool Quay – lift the canal to the Welshpool level. Road access can be obtained at Bank (SJ 260129) and Pool Quay (SJ 255116).

The latter was actually named before the arrival of the canal. Over to the left, beyond the busy main road, was the upper limit of the river Severn navigation. A basin and quay were established here, and there is a record of freight being trans-shipped between cut and river. There were also mills and an abbey in the same area.

• Turn left and walk down to the main road.

This is now known as The Prince of Wales Length to mark the first restored section. Again, much weaving is needed to avoid a change in level, and the main road is often uncomfortably close for those on foot. To Buttington (SJ 241089) where a picnic area has been established. Here are three restored lime kilns; again, evidence of the staple traffic on this canal.

The first restored bridge in Welshpool is at Gallowstree (SJ 235080). This was completed in 1992, an early pay-off from the town's by-pass. Before then, it was the southern limit of the Prince of Wales' restoration. There is little evidence today, but from here to the town centre, the canal was lined with wharves, factories and even the gasworks. One place which no longer survives was quaintly named The Welshpool Company for the Manufacture of Flannel by Steam.

The section from here to the town is where the restoration story began. In 1969, members of the Shropshire Union Canal Society instituted a major clean up of the canal and towing path. It allowed the town to see what a wonderful asset the canal could be, and strongly assisted the objector's case when the original route for the Welshpool by-pass planned to use the line of the canal.

• Welshpool has a wide range of food and refreshment to offer; simply leave the canal at the Canal Wharf and turn right along Severn Street into the centre. At the wharf there is a trip boat which operates a regular service during the summer. It is also the home of Powysland Museum and Canal Centre.

Welshpool Lock (SJ 226073) lifts the canal almost another 6 feet (1.8m) to a straight section, alongside what used to be the A483 until the by-pass was opened. Whitehouse Bridge, restored in 1995, takes the canal away from the noise and fumes towards Belan Locks. The method adopted for constructing this crossing can be seen by the old length of canal, some 100 yards long, now redundant. Also at this point is the entrance to Powis Castle. Now in the care of The National Trust, this medieval building is well worth the detour needed to visit it.

Belan Locks are another fine restoration in exquisite surrounding scenery. A picnic area has been created on what was the old wharf (SJ 215051). Again, there were lime kilns. Still on a hillside, the canal climbs another lock at Brithdir. A pub – The Horseshoe – is conveniently close here, with yet another lime kiln and a picnic area (SJ 200023).

A small aqueduct takes the canal over Luggy Brook (SJ 197021), passes Berriew lock and then on to an embankment before striding out over the second longest aqueduct on the canal at Berriew (SJ 189007).

The main road closes in by Refail as the canal reaches another wharf. There is also a bus garage on the towing path side (SJ 001192). The sloping fields to the right host a huge quantity of wild snowdrop bulbs. Around mid February each year, a carpet of white flowers, those wonderful harbingers of spring, grace the scene.

The next bridge marks the limit of the eastern section, and is where the terminus existed for many years. Although little evidence now remains on the ground, this was a hive of activity during those long years before the western branch opened. Records indicate that there were wharves, warehouses, several lime kilns, a maltings with drying kiln, and housing for those working there (S0 194992).

Immediately at the start of this western section, there is a major road blockage at the Nags Head pub. The old canal bridge originally used by the road is still extant, but the route has taken a left hand deviation to ease what was a sharp right hand bend (SO 990195).

• Bus stop right outside the pub.

Cross the road and take the left hand bend down the B4385 to Montgomery. A few yards along, access to the towpath will be discovered. Again, the road is an increasingly intrusive presence, but the quality of canal architecture more than compensates. Two more flattened bridges are encountered around Ffron (SO 181977 and SO 174972) as the canal moves to the west of the A483 for a spell. There are pretty accommodation bridges with cast-iron railings along this section, the difference to what has gone before a clear indication of its separate pedigree.

The towing path makes a brief diversion to the right bank at Brynderwen, this to accommodate a coal wharf. By the lock here is a restored company warehouse (SO 163955). The pound just before the lock has a superb crop of fish. Encouraged (and fed) by the house owner there and free from the predation of fishermen, they grow to quite a large size.

At SO 159948, the canal passes under a reinstated road bridge at Ardleen. This is the last crossing and there is no path under the bridge; a scramble over the Armco barrier is needed. Traffic moves along this road at a frenetic rate, so great care must be exercised. There was a mill and wharf here before this road was built, now all traces are gone.

Beyond here, the pestilential presence of the road is felt for the last time. Although still sharing the Severn valley, they keep a respectful distance from each other and the canal gains from seclusion and continued fine scenery. A tiny aqueduct spans the river at Aberbechan and leads to the substantial cast-iron Aberbechan Road bridge. A bus stop will be found on the main road 300 yards (274m) to the left.

The Penarth feeder brings a supply of water in from the river Severn close by and the derelict Freestone lock indicates the southernmost extent of the restoration. A footpath continues towards Newtown, and it is possible to pick out the course of the canal for some of this section. The path then diverts from the original line, now host to a sewage works, but joins again for the last 800 yards (730m) to what was the old canal terminus in Newtown.

There are still indications of the area's history with names such as Canal Street and Old Wharf in evidence. A couple of old buildings were once used by the canal, but the feel of this most pretty canal has, by now, gone.

Transport

Crosville service 75 Oswestry to Newtown runs more or less alongside the canal from Llanymynach to Newtown, and can be accessed at the points mentioned, and in Welshpool.

Montgomery Canal Cruises, Severn Street Wharf, Welshpool, Powys SY21 9PQ, operate MALDWYN, a 52-seater trip boat along the canal from Welshpool every day from April to October. This is a 1 hour cruise. Charter trips (minimum 16 passengers) can be arranged in advance, and can last up to 3 hours. Food provided if required. There are also canoes and motor boats available for hire by the hour and a steel narrowboat, rented out by the day. Their contact number is 01938 553271 or 0860 189709.

A 3-day hire aboard CLIFTON, a steel narrow cruiser, is available from Anglo Welsh Holidays. This allows full exploration of the navigable lengths around Welshpool. Their number is 01858 466910.

Tourist Information Services

Mile End Services
Oswestry, Shropshire SY11 4JA
Tel: (01691) 662488.

The Heritage Centre
2 Church Terrace, Oswestry, Shropshire SY11 2TE
Tel: (01691) 662488.

Flash Centre
Salop Road, Welshpool, Powys SY21 7DH
Tel: (01938) 552043.
Central Car Park, Newtown, Powys SY16 2PW
Tel: (01686) 625580.

Maps

Ordnance Survey "Landranger" sheets 126 and 136 cover the whole
line.

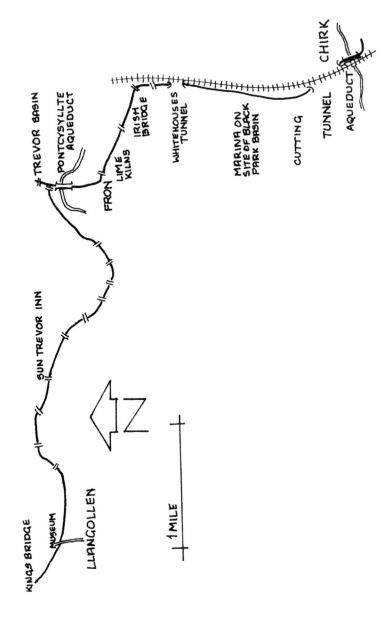

KINGS BRIDGE

MUSEUM

LLANGOLLEN

SUN TREVOR INN

TREVOR BASIN

PONTCYSYLLTE AQUEDUCT

FRON

LIME KILNS

IRISH BRIDGE

WHITEHOUSES TUNNEL

MARINA ON SITE OF BLACK PARK BASIN

CUTTING

TUNNEL

CHIRK

AQUEDUCT

N

1 MILE

12. The Ellesmere (Llangollen) Canal

Then ...

Although most of the canal is in England and thus outside the scope of this book, to understand its pivotal role in the canal story of north Wales, we will look at it in its entirety in this section, limiting only exploration to the Welsh section.

The canal as we know it today is a long way from the one envisaged by the original promoters. The original idea of the canal came from a group of ironmakers in Ruabon. In 1791, encouraged by the explosion of interest in canals, and fearful of being left behind in the competition stakes, they joined forces with local mine owners to propose a canal to Chester and the river Mersey, there to access Liverpool Docks. There would be branches to further ironworks in the Wrexham area en route to the coast, and extensions beyond Ruabon to access limestone at Llanymynech.

Other suggestions for a route were made and eventually William Jessop was called in as a consultant in 1792. His report not only mapped out the line as originally suggested, but had a southwards extension through Chirk to Frankton, then to Weston and Shrewsbury.

There were several major engineering problems. The two biggest were a 4,000-yard tunnel around Ruabon, and an aqueduct over the Dee valley at Pontcysyllte. Not that these discouraged investors. Canal mania was at its height and shares were greatly oversubscribed.

An Act was granted in 1793. There were numerous last minute changes, including one to replace the original plan to use barge locks (14 feet x 70 feet/4.2m x 21.4m) with narrow (7 feet x 70 feet/2.1m x 21.4m) ones. Jessop was appointed Engineer, with William Turner and Thomas

Denson as assistants. But the most enlightened appointment was made a few months later when a young man by the name of Thomas Telford was engaged as "Overlooker of the Works".

Pontcysyllte Aqueduct, Llangollen Canal.

First work was carried out at the northern end from Chester to Netherpool, now re-named Ellesmere Port. This was completed by 1796 and instantly provided income from tolls.

A section from the planned Shrewsbury line near Lower Frankton towards Llanymynech was started in 1794, aimed to connect with the newly enacted Montgomeryshire Canal at Carreghofa – see Chapter Eleven. About this time, the Chirk to Pontcysyllte length was started. The huge gap across the Dee valley was causing some scratching of heads. The original plan for an aqueduct had been modified to some locks down into the valley, thus reducing the height, but this was changed in 1795.

Jessop proposed a radical solution: an iron aqueduct. Exactly how he reached this idea is not documented, but there is good circumstantial evidence to suppose that Telford suggested it. Both men had seen iron in use on a much smaller scale – indeed, Jessop was part owner of an ironworks. He seems to have taken full credit for it at the time, although Telford, later in his life, claimed it for himself. We will never know the truth.

Work started on this mammoth undertaking in 1796, but soon came to a stop. Realising that construction would take a long time, resources were concentrated on the Ceiriog river aqueduct at Chirk. This would allow a link to Lower Frankton, again resulting in toll income.

Telford, meanwhile, was also engaged on re-planning the Chester link. Several changes were incorporated and a new Act obtained in 1796. But events were overtaking the canal. There was a huge flight of locks involved and several conflicting schemes were presented to overcome these. One even included a boat lift.

By the turn of the century, Jessop had noted that new collieries, closer to the river, would provide coal to Chester at a price the canal could not match, and he advised against construction. One very short level length of 2 miles (3.2km) north west of Wrexham was completed and flooded, but boats never used it.

Meanwhile, "back at the ranch", work was under way on the great aqueduct at Pontcysyllte. When completed in 1805, it was 335 yards (306.9m) across the valley and 42 yards (38.6m) above the river. The canal then continued for some 300 yards (274.3m) towards Acrefair where it ended in basins. Tramways served the canal, delivering stone and coal from sites further in the hills.

By this time, the canal was suffering an identity crisis. Much was built, but it didn't really go anywhere. There was trade along the canal although the original concept of serving Ruabon and its ironmakers had been changed. Shrewsbury was still a distant hope, but the Montgomeryshire was open and trading, providing traffic to the Ellesmere.

The company had earlier talked to the Chester Canal company about linking with them. Their line, a barge canal opened from the river Dee in Chester to Nantwich in 1779, was in dire financial straits, and they saw the possibility of trade from a new company as a lifesaver.

And they held a trump card: supplying water for the Ellesmere's Wirral line. Without that, the canal was hopeless. Jessop surveyed eastward and came up with the line for a branch to Whitchurch. This would be extended to Hurleston there to meet the Chester.

But yet another problem arose. Nineteen locks would be needed to complete the extension; that meant a better water supply was needed. There was plenty in the Welsh hills, and to get it, a small channel from Llantisilio to Trevor through Llangollen was planned. That it was decided to make it navigable is something for which every canal enthusiast is eternally grateful.

In the final days of 1805, the Ellesmere finally connected to the outside world. Limestone, timber and coal all flowed along the canal and prosperous times were envisaged. As traffic from the hills to Liverpool and the world had to pass along the Chester route, closer cooperation seemed to make good business and fiscal sense.

The two companies amalgamated on Thursday July 1st 1813, becoming The United Company of Proprietors of the Ellesmere and Chester Canals. There things stood. The line from Lower Frankton towards Shrewsbury had reached Weston Lullingfield by 1805, but never got any further. An attempt to reach Prees had been made but foundered after 3 miles (4.8km) and a short arm into Ellesmere itself had been completed.

The next relevant event to stir corporate lethargy was the announcement in 1825 of plans for a canal to link Birmingham with Liverpool. This was to run from Autherley junction, near Wolverhampton, to make an end-on junction with the old Chester line at Nantwich. The E & C proprietors saw a great opportunity for their trade to be extended towards the industrial heart of England.

But it was a close-run thing. Thomas Telford engineered the line, producing a superb straight canal with locks grouped in flights. It was efficient to work, but had so nearly been laid as a railway. Soon after the first plans were announced, the Railway Age burst upon an unsuspecting England. The "movers and shakers" of the time, ever wanting to be first with the latest toy, made strong representations for a railway, but failed.

The newcomer had lots going for it. The ironmasters around Shrewsbury finally had their canal connection to the outside world as the Newport branch was opened, and the E & C built a 10-mile (16km) branch from Barbridge to Middlewich, there to join the Trent and Mersey and with it, the opportunity to reach Manchester by a more direct route.

But it was a canal built too late. Even before it opened, railways were being announced northwards from Birmingham. This had the effect of ensuring that tolls on the canal could never be at a realistic level.

It opened in 1835. There had been fiendish constructional difficulties and Telford was increasingly less helpful, being overtaken by ill health and old age (he was already in his 68th year when he accepted the commission to build the B & L). William Cubitt, who had worked with Telford on earlier projects, took over in 1833 and Telford died the following year, aged 77. He never saw his last major project completed.

Before many years had passed, the B & L realised that they were in difficulties. They had paid no dividends to their investors and, with the Ellesmere and Chester company so involved with the trade, discussions were instigated that resulted in a merger in 1845.

The Ellesmere and Chester company had obtained an Act in 1845 to allow them to take over the Birmingham and Liverpool Junction canal. Anxious to retain their monopoly on traffic, the company also examined the possibility of railways being introduced. This was achieved, as mentioned in Chapter Eleven.

The original Ellesmere line continued to trade quite well. Collieries and limestone works around Chirk were providing plenty of traffic, but it had dwindled as rail links offered better service. Remarkably, most of the system stayed open. The Weston branch suffered a breach near Dandyford, and the LNWR would not fork out the £14,000 needed to repair it. The furthest section was then abandoned and a new terminus established at Hordley, less than a mile from Lower Frankton.

The last commercial trade on the old E & C system was recorded just before the last war. In 1944, heartened by the chance of getting an abandonment Act through whilst the country's collective mind was elsewhere, the LMS Railway listed no less than 175 miles (281.6km) of canal they wanted to close.

Everything around the Shrewsbury area was included, the Montgomery, both the Llanymynech and Weston branches together with the Ellesmere, Whitchurch and Prees branches. The saving grace for the Llantisilio to Hurleston Junction line was its role as a water channel. This was regularised in 1955 when the South Cheshire Water Board formally agreed with BW for the supply of water to their Hurleston reservoir.

Spot, power for the horse-drawn trip boat from Llangollen to Llantisilio.

By this time, the earliest signs of a leisure interest were taking hold. Navigation was restored and this line has subsequently become the most popular canal cruising line in the country.

It was also about this time that British Waterways decided on a name change. They established a small hire fleet in Chester and realised that the E & C would be quite a draw. But the name didn't have a good ring to it; "Llangollen" was altogether more evocative so that is what it became. BW erected signs to that effect, and thus it is popularly known. Those with a longer canal pedigree still tend to refer to it as "The Welsh Canal" or "The Llangollen Branch".

And Now ...

For all its Welsh nomenclature, the canal is only in the country for 11 of its 46 miles (17.7km of 74km); this in two sections.

The first, a mere 2½ miles (4km), is around the village of Bettisfield where the border has a little kick south. Heading west, this starts at SJ 481355 and finishes as England asserts itself again at SJ 455350. There is no public transport in the area, but the towing path is in fine condition for walking.

The tiny village of Bettisfield is central to this section. There is a small shop canalside together with a boat builder, proudly displaying the Welsh flag. Beyond the boatyard, the canal returns to gently rolling countryside with the canal passing under a road bridge before sweeping left. The border is now on the right, crossing the water as the canal makes a sharp right, clinging to the contour. There are no markers to indicate this "state line".

The river Ceiriog is the main border the canal crosses. From then, it's Wales all the way. The Horseshoe Falls at Llantisilio some 11 miles (18.2km) away. There is a bus from Chirk to Llangollen, allowing a one-way walk over the section.

An ideal starting point for this exploration is actually on the English side. The small post office at Chirk Bank – the only Welsh office in England – offers basic refreshment and the chance to park (SJ 292371). Note the unusual canal channel: a concrete trough.

This section of the canal, together with much of the line between Trevor and Llangollen has suffered chronic instability for years. After a catastrophic failure near Sun Trevor in 1984, money was made available both to repair that and to investigate the rest of the suspect area.

Over the next decade, the canal was systematically upgraded and further failure is now most unlikely. Whilst the concrete is something of an eyesore, it will mellow. Don't forget that canals everywhere once bore construction scars. Now they have melded with the scenery, been taken over by wild life, looking as if they have existed for ever.

After a few yards, the canal turns sharp right. This is Chirk Aqueduct. It's an impressive structure, and must have been more so before the

Pontcysyllte Aqueduct, Llangollen Canal.

railway one alongside and higher took some of its glory away. At the far end is Chirk Tunnel, 459 yards/419.7m. There is a good towing path through with a protective rail between you and the water. A torch is handy, or a boat will light the way for you. It is then possible to see how much water runs down the canal.

It is usual to experience little or no flow on a canal, but this one, being a water supply first and foremost, tends to run quite swiftly through here where the flow is constricted. You will soon outpace any boat. There is a road link over the top for those who tend towards claustrophobia.

The cutting beyond is exquisitely beautiful, falling gently back to water level as it rounds a right hand bend. Beyond, a winding hole marks what was once Black Park Basin. This was a rail/canal interchange point. A narrow-gauge railway used to deliver slate and granite from quarries further up the valley, and coal from local collieries. There is now little evidence of what was once a vibrant industrial scene some 60 years ago.

A huge leisure development now dominates the scenery, the centrepiece of which is a marina with a hire-boat base. Soon, Whitehouses tunnel appears. This is only a short one – 190 yards/173.6m – and is not too forbidding. Soon after leaving this tunnel, the canal turns sharp left at Irish Bridge. On this corner was once a large rail siding where limestone from Pen-y-Graig quarry was loaded by the Great Western Railway.

The quarry itself is further along the canal, on the left. They used the canal in earlier days, but much of this trade was lost when the railway arrived. The lime kilns were operating until the last war. It was then decided that they were a beacon from the air, and the strategically vital steelworks in Wrexham were only a few minutes away in a Luftwaffe bomber.

The canal is now contained in a concrete trough. A lift bridge at Fron heralds a right turn leading to the Pontcysyllte Aqueduct.

This structure has had superlatives hurled at it from anyone who can lift a pen, and every one fully justified. If vertigo rather than claustrophobia is your curse, there is a road alternative. Leave the towpath at Fron, heading left towards the main road. Here, a right turn signposted Trevor, drops down the Dee valley and up the other side to Trevor Basin.

• A bus runs along the main road here.

At the far end of the aqueduct is the Basin and a low bridge to the left under which the canal arrives from Llangollen. There is a wooden footbridge over the canal which gives access to a hire company's shop and, through the gate, to the continuation of the walk.

Alternatively, carry on to the next road bridge, turn left to the road and left again. This takes the walk past The Telford Inn before meeting up with the short cut.

• Walk up to the main road and a bus to Llangollen can be caught.

Pick up the canal again by the road bridge, with the towing path on the right. This crosses after a few yards and stays to the left for the rest of the walk. The term "contour canal" is now re-defined. It sticks rigidly to the north side of the Dee valley and contorts itself dramatically in so doing.

Ahead is Castell Dinas Brân, 1100 thrombosis-inducing feet (335m) up in the hills. Here, Eliseg, Prince of Powys, defended his land against the English invaders. Today, they are called visitors and Eliseg's descendants welcome them with open cash registers.

Sun Trevor Inn marks the start of a very narrow section with a blind bend. It's a good spot for those with a sadistic streak to watch often inexperienced boaters meeting and trying to cope with a perceptible current whilst meeting other boats. A couple of bank failures in the 1940s occurred here. One released sufficient debris and water to take out the railway track below. A goods train was wrecked, sadly resulting in fatal injuries to the driver.

High above the rooftops, the Llangollen Canal reaches the town. This walking section finishes here by bridge 45.

• Leave the canal, turn left down the hill, over the river and into Llangollen for the return bus.

But there are still 1½ miles (2.4km) left. The old warehouse on the wharf once housed a very informative canal museum. This recently transferred to a part of the 'Dr Who' exhibition nearby and is well worth a call. There is no regular public transport to the far end, but the Llangollen Steam Railway have a station at Berwyn close by that can be used during their periods of operation. Or perhaps you've walked enough.

In that case, there are horse-drawn trip boats that will convey you to the source of the water at Horseshoe Falls. These operate from the wharf frequently, from early to late season. Trips from here have been available since 1884; a very early pleasure use for the canal.

The field to the right, soon after the start, is where the world famous Llangollen Eisteddfod is held. The railway below on the left crosses the river, and a bridge crosses the canal. This is Pentrefelin bridge where a wharf was once located. In about 1852, a tramway was laid high into the hills. From there, slate and stone were brought down to be carried away by boat. This lasted until the turn of the century, and was probably the last traffic this high up the canal.

The feeder continues in its narrow trough until Kings Bridge is reached. Here, the towing path looks down on the Chain Bridge Hotel which is a lot prettier from the front. The train station and bridge which gives its name to the hotel can also be seen.

The valve house controlling the flow of water into the canal is located right alongside the Horseshoe Falls, so named because of its shape. It was built in 1947 and is the point where canal and river finally meet.

Maps

Ordnance Survey "Landranger" series sheets 117, 125 and 126 are needed to cover all this canal.

Transport

Operated by Bryn Melin, details on 01978 860828 (not Sundays).

Caution

There are 2 tunnels and 1 high aqueduct; sufferers from vertigo or claustrophobia should take note. A torch for use in the tunnels is a useful accessory.

Tourist Information

Town Hall, Castle Street, Llangollen, Denighshire LL20 5PD
Tel: (01978) 860828.

The Llangollen Canal near Sun Trevor. The channel has been rebuilt here following numerous landslips.